Swimming

Other titles in the Science Behind Sports series:

Swimming

LIZABETH HARDMAN

LUCENT BOOKS
A part of Gale, Cengage Learning

GALE
CENGAGE Learning™

Detroit • New York • San Francisco • New Haven, Conn • Waterville, Maine • London

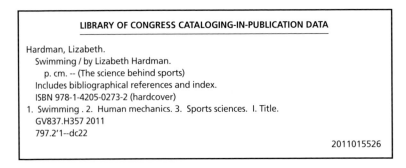

LIBRARY OF CONGRESS CATALOGING-IN-PUBLICATION DATA

Hardman, Lizabeth.
  Swimming / by Lizabeth Hardman.
    p. cm. -- (The science behind sports)
  Includes bibliographical references and index.
  ISBN 978-1-4205-0273-2 (hardcover)
  1. Swimming . 2. Human mechanics. 3. Sports sciences. I. Title.
  GV837.H357 2011
  797.2'1--dc22

                                                  2011015526

Lucent Books
27500 Drake Rd
Farmington Hills MI 48331

ISBN-13: 978-1-4205-0273-2
ISBN-10: 1-4205-0273-5

Printed in the United States of America
1 2 3 4 5 6 7 15 14 13 12 11
Printed by Bang Printing, Brainerd, MN, 1st Ptg., 08/2011

TABLE OF CONTENTS

On March 21, 1970, Slovenian ski jumper Vinko Bogataj took a terrible fall while competing at the Ski-flying World Championships in Oberstdorf, West Germany. Bogataj's pinwheeling crash was caught on tape by an ABC *Wide World of Sports* film crew and eventually became synonymous with "the agony of defeat" in competitive sporting. While many viewers were transfixed by the severity of Bogataj's accident, most were not aware of the biomechanical and environmental elements behind the skier's fall—heavy snow and wind conditions that made the ramp too fast and Bogataj's inability to maintain his center of gravity and slow himself down. Bogataj's accident illustrates that, no matter how mentally and physically prepared an athlete may be, scientific principles—such as momentum, gravity, friction, and aerodynamics—always have an impact on performance.

Lucent Books's Science Behind Sports series explores these and many more scientific principles behind some of the most popular team and individual sports, including baseball, hockey, gymnastics, wrestling, swimming, and skiing. Each volume in the series focuses on one sport or group of related sports. The volumes open with a brief look at the featured sport's origins, history and changes, then move on to cover the biomechanics and physiology of playing, related health and medical concerns, and the causes and treatment of sports-related injuries.

In addition to learning about the arc behind a curve ball, the impact of centripetal force on a figure skater, or how water buoyancy helps swimmers, Science Behind Sports readers will also learn how exercise, training, warming up, and diet and nutrition directly relate to peak performance and enjoyment of the sport. Volumes may also cover why certain sports are popular, how sports function in the business world, and which hot sporting issues—sports doping and cheating, for example—are in the news.

Basic physical science concepts, such as acceleration, kinetics, torque, and velocity, are explained in an engaging and accessible manner. The full-color text is augmented by fact boxes, sidebars, photos, and detailed diagrams, charts and graphs. In addition, a subject-specific glossary, bibliography and index provide further tools for researching the sports and concepts discussed throughout Science Behind Sports.

CHAPTER 1

A Sport for the Ages

I t was 480 B.C. Naval forces of the Persian Empire, under the command of Emperor Xerxes I, had invaded Greece for the second time, hoping to expand their empire. In two battles, the Greek navy, heavily outnumbered, had been soundly defeated by the Persians. But the Greek general Themistocles somehow persuaded his sailors to engage the Persians one more time. Xerxes, too, was anxious for a final battle that would finish his conquest once and for all.

The Greeks managed to get the Persian navy to sail into the narrow Straits of Salamis, where their hundreds of ships became so crowded that they could not maneuver. The Greeks took advantage of this and sunk or captured over two hundred Persian ships. It marked a turning point in the struggle between Greece and Persia. After more defeats the next year, the Persians made no more attempts to invade Greece.

In his most famous work, *The Histories*, Greek historian Herodotus (484–425 B.C.) describes the battle:

> There fell in this combat Ariabignes, one of the chief commanders of the fleet, who was … brother of Xerxes; and with him perished a vast number of men of high repute, Persians, Medes, and allies. Of the Greeks there died only a few; for, as they were able to swim,

all those that were not slain outright by the enemy escaped from the sinking vessels and swam across to Salamis. But on the side of the barbarians [the Persians] more perished by drowning than in any other way, since they did not know how to swim.[1]

The Persians lost the Battle of Salamis and ultimately the conquest of Greece, in part because they could not swim.

A Useful Activity

Today, people swim for many reasons. First, swimming is a very popular form of recreation. It can be very relaxing to spend some time in a swimming pool filled with cool water on a hot day. Swimming provides an opportunity for family and friends of all ages to socialize and have fun by engaging in an activity that they can enjoy together.

Swimming has significant health benefits. It is an excellent form of aerobic exercise. It requires the use of a lot of oxygen, so the heart and lungs are given a good workout, and muscles are strengthened and toned. Swimming burns a lot of calories, which can help a person to maintain a healthy

A family enjoys a fun day in a swimming pool. In addition to its recreational aspects, swimming is popular for its health benefits and as a competitive sport.

weight. Water supports the weight of the body, so there is very little stress on the joints, which makes swimming a good choice for the elderly or those with disabilities who wish to exercise. Swimming is also commonly used as a form of rehabilitation for athletes with injuries.

Competitive swimming is a very popular sport, especially at world-class events such as the Summer Olympics. Today's competitions include races of varying lengths, for both individuals and teams, using several different types of swimming strokes. There are also competitions in diving; open-water racing, such as triathlons; and in team sports, such as water polo and synchronized swimming.

Swimming is also a needed skill for several occupations. Lifeguards at pools and beaches must be excellent swimmers and have a thorough grasp of rescue swimming techniques. Swimming and diving are used by biologists and environmentalists to study aquatic plants and animals in their natural habitat. Some forms of entertainment, such as water ballet, require swimming skills.

Swimming Strokes

There are four main kinds of swimming strokes, or styles, used in swimming, particularly competitive swimming: the front crawl, or freestyle; the breaststroke; the backstroke; and the butterfly. All four are made up of five general parts: the arm stroke, the leg kick, breathing techniques, coordination of the movements of the body parts, and the position of the body in relation to the surface of the water.

The front crawl, also sometimes called the Australian crawl or freestyle, is the stroke most familiar to recreational swimmers. In the front crawl, the body is aligned face down (prone) in the water with the arms extended forward and the legs extended straight back. The head is kept face down except when it is turned to the side to take a breath. The front crawl combines an alternating overarm stroke with an up-and-down flutter kick. The upper body rolls slightly from side to side while doing the front crawl. Because both arms and legs are constantly moving, the front crawl is the fastest of the four strokes.

THE BUTTERFLY STROKE

The butterfly stroke, developed in the 1930s, is often considered the most technically challenging swimming stroke. A successful butterfly stroke requires precise coordination and careful timing, as the arms move up and out of the water at the same time, and the legs are held together in a "dolphin kick."

Keep your head down.

Throw both arms over the water in front of your shoulders and pull hands towards your thighs.

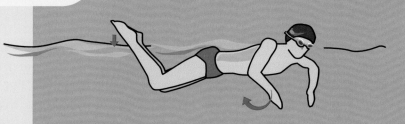

Breathe in quickly when your hands are almost at your thighs.

Kick your legs down as your hands come out of the water.

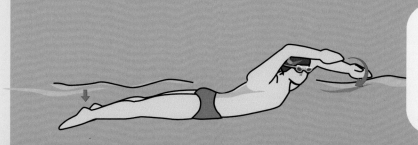

Kick your legs down as your hands go in the water.

STARTING BLOCK

20 miles
The distance elephants can swim in one day, using their trunks like snorkels to breathe under water.

The breaststroke is also done in the prone position. For this stroke, the arm movement begins with the arms extended forward with the palms together. Then the hands turn outward and move apart (the out sweep). They then point downward and push the water backward (the in sweep). At the end of the in sweep the hands then come back together and push forward to the beginning position (the recovery). As the arms come forward, the upper body is raised out of the water to take a breath. The leg movement is often called a frog kick. First, the feet are pulled in toward the body with the knees together. The legs are then separated wide, then brought together very quickly to push the water backward. For the breaststroke, the leg kick provides most of the thrust that propels the swimmer forward.

The backstroke, as the name implies, is done on the back and is similar to the front crawl. It is the only one of the four strokes that begins with the swimmer in the water rather than on the side of the pool. The arm movement is an overarm movement, and the leg movement is a flutter kick. The arms provide most of the propulsion for the backstroke, with the leg kick important for stabilizing the body in the water.

The butterfly, or fly, is considered by many swimmers to be the most difficult of the strokes, because it is physically demanding and because it is so unforgiving. Any lapse in technique interferes significantly with performance. In the butterfly, the arms begin extended straight out, then move at the same time downward toward the waist, pulling the water backward (the pull) and on toward the hip or thigh, pushing the water back (the push). During the push, the body rises somewhat and a breath is taken. The arms are then brought out of the water and extended forward to begin the next stroke. At the same time, the legs move in a kick called a dolphin kick. The legs are kept together and moved up and down, resembling the way a dolphin's tail looks when it is swimming.

An Ancient Activity

Because of its versatility and wide range of purposes, swimming has been an important human activity throughout history. There are accounts of humans swimming since prehistoric times. In southwestern Egypt, near the border with Libya, is the Cave of Swimmers, discovered by Hungarian explorer László Almásy in 1933. The cave features paintings on the rock walls of what is believed to be people swimming. The paintings date to the time of the most recent Ice Age, about ten thousand years ago. Almásy concluded from these paintings that the climate in the Sahara was much different then from the hot, dry climate that exists there today. According to the Egyptian State Information Service website,

> swimming was the favorite sport of the ancient Egyptians, who made use of the River Nile to practice it. The Nile was not the only place for swimming contests. Noblemen's palaces had swimming pools in which princes learnt the sport. The calm waters of the Nile encouraged youths to hold swimming competitions in which they could show their skills.[2]

A 3,000-year-old wall carving from the Assyrian empire shows archers chasing swimmers in the Euphrates River. Other depictions of swimming activities have been found in ancient drawings and cave paintings.

In ancient times, clay seals with images carved on them were used to identify and protect personal property such as a tomb or the contents of a pottery jar. An Egyptian clay seal, estimated to be between six thousand and ten thousand years old, shows four swimmers. Swimmers are also depicted in ancient Babylonian wall carvings, called bas-reliefs, and drawings from the Assyrian Empire.

Written records also indicate that swimming was practiced among ancient peoples. Ancient works of literature, such as the *Epic of Gilgamesh* (Mesopotamia, approximately 2000 B.C.), the *Iliad* and the *Odyssey* (Greek, 800 B.C.), *Beowulf* (Old English, A.D. 700 to 1100), and the Bible, all contain references to swimming. Swimming was considered a necessary skill for ancient Greek and Roman warriors. The Romans built pools and bathhouses throughout their empire, both as social gathering places and for exercise. The Roman emperor Julius Caesar (100–44 B.C.) was known for his swimming skill. Greek philosopher Plato (429 B.C.–347 B.C.) considered a man uneducated if he did not know how to swim.

Swimming in the Middle Ages

During the Middle Ages, from about A.D. 500 to about A.D. 1500, swimming continued to be an important skill for European knights, including swimming while wearing armor. The European emperor Charlemagne (742–814) was known as an excellent swimmer. In Japan, Samurai warriors were also taught to swim while wearing heavy armor and how to stay on their horses in deep water.

Among the nonmilitary population, however, swimming began to lose popularity as water became associated with the transmission of diseases, such as plague. As the Middle Ages drew to a close and the Catholic Church became more of an influence on society, standards of behavior became more conservative and modest, and swimming, which had traditionally been done in the nude, was opposed by the church and continued to decline in popularity.

The first book written especially about swimming is *Colymbetes*, published in 1539 by German professor Nicolas Wynman. Wynman's purpose in writing the book was to help people avoid drowning. It includes a detailed method for learning how to swim using the breaststroke, which was the standard swimming stroke of the time. It also describes flotation devices, such as cow bladders filled with air and belts made of cork. In 1587, British professor Everard Digby wrote a short work about swimming titled *De arte natandi* (The Art of Swimming). In this work, which contains over forty illustrations of various swimming methods and is written in Latin, Digby asserts that humans have the ability to swim better than fish.

Swimming in the Modern Era

After the sixteenth century, swimming began to regain popularity as a pastime. The first known national swimming organization was established in Japan in 1603. In 1696, a French version of Digby's book was published. The book remained very popular for many years, and an English version was read by American statesman and founding father Benjamin Franklin. Franklin is credited with inventing swim fins in 1716 at the age of ten and also with designing a set of hand paddles. In his autobiography, he

The Sutro Baths in San Francisco, California, was one of several public swimming facilities that opened in the United States in the late 1800s.

writes, "I learnt early to swim well. I made two oval Palettes, each about ten inches long and six abroad, with Hole for the Thumbs to hold them tightly in each hand, like Painter's Palettes. In swimming I would hold them edgewise for forward and on the flat Side to draw them back. … They helped me swim much faster but fatigued my Wrist."[3] For his innovations, Benjamin Franklin was admitted into the International Swimming Hall of Fame in Fort Lauderdale, Florida, in 1968.

In seventeenth-century Europe, swimming was still done infrequently, and a "swim" was little more than a dip in the water. As swimming gained popularity in the 1700s, however, public swimming spas began to appear in France and England, and clothing for both men and women designed specifically for swimming was created. As swimming continued to become more popular throughout the 1800s, swimming pools were built in London, England, and other cities in Europe, and competitions organized by the National Swimming Society were held in London. The Amateur Swimming Association of Great Britain was established in 1880 and soon had over three hundred members.

Swimming also became more popular in America. In 1827, the first American swimming school was established by Francis Lieber, and in 1872, the first organized lifeguard service was established at the beach in Atlantic City, New Jersey. City swimming pools began to appear in the 1880s, including a group of pools in San Francisco, California, called the Sutro Baths that included one freshwater pool, five saltwater pools, and one large "ocean" pool that was filled by the high tide. Swimsuits made of wool were available to rent for the day.

The Beginnings of Competitive Swimming

Swimming competitions can be traced back as far as two thousand years ago, when the Japanese held competitive swimming races as early as 36 B.C. Competitive swimming in Europe began in England in the early 1800s. The breaststroke was the most commonly used stroke, as Europeans considered splashing around in the water to be unseemly and this stroke kept the arms and legs mostly under the water.

In 1844 a swimming competition was held in London, to which competitors from several nations were invited to participate. Among the competitors were Flying Gull and Tobacco, Native Americans of the Ojibwa tribe. The Ojibwa used a swimming stroke that looked much like the modern front crawl. The Europeans considered the stroke undignified and would not use it. One observer noted that the stroke was "totally un-European," criticizing the Ojibwa because they "thrashed the water violently with their arms, like sails of a windmill, and beat downward with their feet, blowing with force and forming grotesque antics."[4] When Flying Gull swam the 130-foot (40m) length of the pool in thirty seconds, however, the Europeans were amazed. The Ojibwa soundly defeated the Europeans at the competition with their "undignified" style.

Europeans continued to use only the breaststroke until 1873, when John Arthur Trudgen introduced his version of the front crawl to England. His version, called the trudgen, used an overhead arm motion along with a scissors-like leg kick, similar to the leg kick a frog uses to propel itself forward. In 1901, swimmer F.V.C. Lane used the trudgen to swim 100 yards (91m) in one minute, beating the record using the breaststroke by ten seconds. Because of its greatly superior speed, the trudgen quickly caught on throughout Europe, despite its less-dignified appearance.

The trudgen was later improved by Australian Richmond Cavill. Cavill changed the scissor kick to a flutter kick, in which the legs move up and down, similar to the technique used by Flying Gull and Tobacco in 1844. His version came to be known as the Australian crawl. At the 1902 International Swimming Championships in England, he used his stroke to beat all swimmers still using the trudgen, covering 100 yards (91m) in fifty-eight seconds. In 1922, American swimming sensation Johnny Weissmuller used the Australian crawl and became the first person to swim 109 yards (100m) in under one minute.

STARTING BLOCK

62 feet, 6 inches

The depth reached by William Dickey in the short-lived "plunge for distance" event at the 1904 Olympics.

The Ocean's Seven

In mountain climbing, the Seven Summits is a goal achieved when a climber has reached the summit of the highest mountain on each of the seven continents. The Ocean's Seven is the open-water swimming version of the Seven Summits. To complete the Ocean's Seven, a swimmer must successfully swim across the Irish Channel between Ireland and Scotland, the Cook Strait between New Zealand's north and south islands, the English Channel between France and England, the Molokai Channel between the Hawaiian islands of Oahu and Molokai, the Tsugaru Strait between the Japanese islands of Hokkaido and Honshu, the Catalina Channel off Los Angeles, California, and the Strait of Gibraltar between Spain and northern Africa.

In order to complete the Ocean's Seven, a swimmer must be able to swim long distances in very cold and very warm water, endure strong currents and wind patterns, and have the psychological strength to overcome the physical challenges. The swimmer must also commit to years of planning and take on considerable financial expense.

As of March 2010, 274 mountain climbers have achieved the Seven Summits. As of 2010, no swimmer has yet successfully completed the Ocean's Seven, although several swimmers have completed at least four of the seven swims.

Swimming at the Olympics

Four swimming events—the 100, 500, and 1200 meter freestyle and a 100 meter event for sailors—were included in the first modern Olympic Games, held in April 1896 in Athens, Greece. The first gold medal in swimming was won by Hungarian Alfréd Hajós in the 100 meter freestyle. There was no pool; the competitors were taken out into the ice cold water of the Bay of Zea by boat, and they had to swim back to shore. The next Olympic Games, held in 1900 in Paris, featured seven swimming events, including the 200m, 1000m, 4000m freestyle, a 200m backstroke, a 200m team event, a swimming

Medalists in the 100 meter freestyle competition pose poolside at the 1912 Olympic Games in Stockholm, Sweden, the first Olympic Games to feature women's swimming events.

obstacle course in the Seine River, and an underwater swimming event. Water polo was also added. In 1904, a "plunge for distance" event was added, in which the person who went the deepest after diving into the water was the winner.

Women were not allowed to compete in the Olympics at first, because they were considered too delicate for competitive sports, and swimming would require them to wear swimming attire that was considered too revealing. Two women's swimming events were eventually added to the Stockholm, Sweden, Olympics in 1912. The first American women's team participated at the 1920 games and won all the events. Today, the Summer Olympics features seventeen swimming events for men and seventeen for women. The 2008 games in Beijing, China, added a 10-kilometer (6.2-mile), open-water marathon event for both men and women.

Competitive swimming became more formalized in 1908 with the establishment of the world swimming association Fédération Internationale de Natation Amateur (FINA). Its main objectives are to promote swimming as international competition, to promote international relations, to provide and enforce uniform rules and regulations for competition, to organize international competitive events, and to increase the number of swimming venues around the world. FINA sponsored the first world swimming championship in 1973 in Belgrade, Yugoslavia. Today, over two hundred national swimming associations are members of FINA. In addition to indoor pool racing events, FINA is the governing body for open-water swimming, diving, synchronized swimming, and water polo.

Swimming at the Paralympics

Paralympic swimming is competitive swimming designed for people with disabilities such as limb loss, visual or hearing impairments, spinal cord injuries, cerebral palsy, or dwarfism. The first organized event for disabled athletes that coincided with the Olympics was held in 1948 and was called the 1948 International Wheelchair Games. It was open only to disabled military veterans. In 1960, the event was opened to all athletes, and four hundred athletes from twenty-three countries participated. In 2008, over thirty-nine hundred athletes from 146 countries attended.

The Summer Paralympic Games are held every four years, in the same years and in the same cities as the Summer Olympics. Swimming has been included in the games since their beginning. There are events for both men and women. While competing, participants are not allowed to use any kind of assistive device, such as a prosthetic limb. In addition to the Paralympics, there are dozens of other events for disabled swimmers in the United States and around the world. The International Paralympic Committee is the governing body which makes the rules for the sport.

Swimmers compete at the 2008 Paralympic Games in Beijing, China.

Open-Water Swimming

Open-water swimming is swimming in natural bodies of water rather than in swimming pools. Open-water swimming offers unique challenges: cold water, choppy water, waves, bad weather, tides and currents, and aquatic wildlife. Many swimmers enjoy it and compete in it, however, and there are few bodies of water in the world that have not been crossed, including the Atlantic Ocean.

"Open water swimming can be a wonderful activity," says open-water enthusiast John F. Walker. "Open water swimming is to pool swimming as trail running is to track running. It is a chance to get out and simply enjoy your surroundings. You can stretch out your stroke and get into a rhythm that you can't achieve when there are walls every 25 or 50 meters."[5]

One of the most frequently crossed bodies of water is the English Channel, a part of the Atlantic Ocean that separates England and France. At its narrowest point, it is 22 miles (35km) across. In 1872, J.B. Johnson attempted to swim across the Channel to France, but he gave up after only one hour. Three years later, Paul Boyton made it across, but he was wearing a special suit designed for flotation. That same year, Matthew Webb became the first person to swim unaided across the English Channel. He finished the swim in twenty-one hours, forty-five minutes and was met on the French side by thousands of cheering people.

In 1926, nineteen-year-old American Olympic swimmer Gertrude Ederle became the first woman to swim the Channel. The morning of her swim, the *London Daily News* asserted that "even the most uncompromising champion of the rights and capacities of women must admit that in contests of physical skill, speed, and endurance they must remain forever the weaker sex."[6] Ederle completed the crossing in only fourteen hours and thirty-one minutes, breaking the existing men's record by over two hours. In 2007, sixty-year-old Englishwoman Linda Ashmore became the oldest woman to swim the Channel. She recalls,

AN AMAZING FEAT

Since it was first crossed by Captain Matthew Webb in 1875, the English Channel has become one of the world's premier swimming challenges. Because of the Channel's tides, crossing times can vary widely, from 7 hours to over 25 hours. Despite dozens of crossings each year, only six fatalities have been recorded in the 135 years since Webb's crossing.

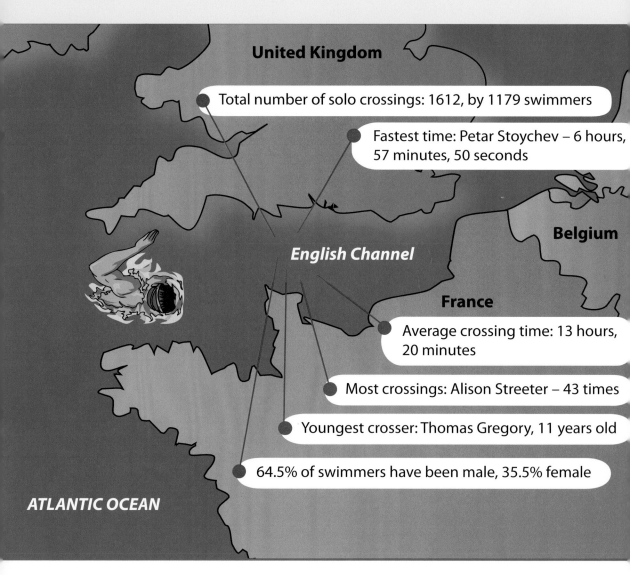

United Kingdom

Total number of solo crossings: 1612, by 1179 swimmers

Fastest time: Petar Stoychev – 6 hours, 57 minutes, 50 seconds

Belgium

English Channel

France

Average crossing time: 13 hours, 20 minutes

Most crossings: Alison Streeter – 43 times

Youngest crosser: Thomas Gregory, 11 years old

64.5% of swimmers have been male, 35.5% female

ATLANTIC OCEAN

"It was a beautiful day, and there were no clouds in the sky … the first eleven to twelve hours were great and I thoroughly enjoyed it, but the last bit was quite horrendous. I just had to swim stroke by stroke to get to the other side.… I was always pretty determined. As long as my arms were still moving and working, I was going to keep going.… Don't tell anyone but I am thinking of doing it again when I am 65![7]

The longest open-water swim took place in 1998, when Frenchman Benoit Lecomte swam across the Atlantic Ocean, a distance of 3,480 miles (5,601km) in seventy-two days. He swam for six to eight hours each day, accompanied by two sailors. Today, FINA sponsors world–class, open-water championship events, such as the Open Water Grand Prix and the Junior Open Water Swimming World Championships.

Gertrude Ederle

Gertrude Ederle was born October 23, 1905, in Manhattan, New York, the daughter of a German butcher, who taught her to swim at a young age. At thirteen she joined the Women's Swimming Association and was soon breaking many amateur swimming records. At seventeen she went to the 1924 Olympics and won a gold medal in the 4x100 meter relay and two bronze medals in the 100m and 400m freestyle. Her first experience with open-water swimming came in 1925 when she swam 21 miles (34km) over seven hours across New York Bay from Manhattan to Sandy Hook, New Jersey.

Later that year she made her first attempt to swim the English Channel, but she failed. On August 26, 1926, she tried again, entering the water at Cap Gris-Nez, France, at 7:05 A.M. and completing the trip successfully in fourteen hours and thirty-one minutes. Ederle was the first woman to ever swim the Channel. Her time, which was faster than any men's time to that point, stood as the record until 1950. It is said that the first person to greet her when she crawled out of the water was a British immigration officer, who asked to see her passport.

In 1933 Ederle fell down some stairs, injuring her spine. She did not swim again, but she was able to teach swimming to children. She was inducted into the International Swimming Hall of Fame in Fort Lauderdale, Florida, in 1965. Ederle died on November 30, 2003, at the age of ninety-eight.

Diving

The origins of competitive diving began in the seventeenth century in Germany and Sweden, when gymnasts adapted their sport to the water. Interest in competitive diving rose in the late 1800s, at about the same time as the rise in popularity of competitive swimming. The first diving club, called Neptun, was begun in Germany in 1882. Official rules governing the sport were written in 1891. Early competitions included both springboard diving and platform diving, but at the time there was only one kind of dive: the common head first dive used by most swimmers. In England and the United States, bridge diving became popular but was later abandoned because of a high number of accidents and serious injuries.

Men's platform diving was added to the Summer Olympics in 1904, with springboard diving added in 1908. In 1928 the FINA International Diving Committee was established and divided diving into five events for the springboard and six for the platform, a structure still used today. The committee also established four body positions for competition: the straight-in dive, the pike (the body is flexed at the hip with the knees straight), the tuck (both hips and knees are flexed with hands on the knees or shins), and the free position, which allows the diver to add more complicated movements in the air, such as twists. German and Swedish divers dominated the sport during its first two decades, with American divers taking over after 1920. In 2000, synchronized diving, in which two divers perform the same dive together, was added, the first new swimming event added since 1920. Today there are sixty-three dives for the 1-meter (3.3-foot) springboard, sixty-seven for the 3-meter (9.8-foot) springboard, and eighty-five dives for platform.

Synchronized Swimming

Synchronized swimming is a combination of swimming, ballet, and gymnastics. Routines may be performed by an individual swimmer, a duet (two swimmers), a trio (three swimmers), or a team and involves a choreographed set of complex movements in the water set to music. A routine

lasts from two to five minutes, depending on how many swimmers are participating. Routines are judged based on technical skill, the difficulty of the movements and how precisely and together, or "in sync," the swimmers perform them, and on artistic interpretation, the variety of movements, their patterns, the use of the pool space, and how well the movements reflect the tone of the music. Synchronized swimming routines involve difficult movements, such as lifts and throws, and swimmers are not allowed to touch the bottom or sides of the pool, so it requires strength and flexibility. Since a lot of time is spent under the water, it also requires good breath control and aerobic endurance.

The first synchronized swimming competition was held in 1891 in Berlin, Germany, and, like diving, it became more popular along with competitive swimming. The first North American competition was held in 1924 in Montreal, Canada. Synchronized swimming gained a great deal of attention in the 1940s and 1950s, when swimming champion Esther Williams introduced the sport to millions in Hollywood movies. Synchronized swimming was demonstrated

Japan's national synchronized swimming team performs a routine at a competition. Synchronized swimming became an official Olympic sport in 1984.

at the 1952 Olympics but was not recognized as an official water sport until FINA adopted it in 1968. It became an official Olympic sport for women in 1984. Today's competitions include only duets and teams.

Water Polo

Water polo is a team water sport. Each team has seven players including a goalkeeper. It is very much like soccer or ice hockey in that the object is to score points by getting a ball into the opposing team's net. The game is divided into four periods, which, at the Olympic level, last eight minutes each. The winner is the team that has scored the most goals by the end of the fourth period.

Water polo, a team sport similar to ice hockey or soccer, demands great strength and stamina from its players.

Water polo requires strength and stamina, because the players must move back and forth between the goals, 21 to 27 yards (19m to 23m) at a time, against the resistance of the water. When a player is not actively involved in the play, he or she must tread water and is not allowed to touch the

bottom of the pool. Water polo is also a very high-contact, aggressive sport, involving a lot of pushing and pulling on opposing players. Sharp reflexes and an ability to focus are necessary because of the rapid pace of the game. Water polo also requires good hand-eye coordination, because players are only allowed to catch or throw the ball with one hand at a time, and passing the ball effectively to teammates can make the difference between winning and losing.

Water polo originally evolved from rugby football, a popular team sport in England and Scotland, and was played in rivers or lakes. At that time, the "ball" was made from a pig stomach. In the 1860s, a rubber ball was designed for water polo. (The word *polo* is the English pronunciation of the Indian word *pulu*, meaning "ball.") Official rules for water polo were written by the London Swimming Club in 1870.

CHAPTER 2

Training and Conditioning

Competitive swimming requires muscle strength and power, endurance, flexibility, and speed. As with any competitive sport, swimming requires that a great deal of time be devoted to training and conditioning practices that develop these abilities. Training and conditioning activities for swimming are done both in the pool and in the gym. In addition to training activities, proper diet and nutrition are critical for successful competitors.

Training for Strength and Power

Muscle strength, especially upper body strength, is crucial for competitive swimmers, because it improves speed, endurance, and power, which are all necessary for success in competition. Strength training is done by working the muscles against some kind of resistance: a handheld barbell or dumbbell, a weight machine, a weighted ball called a medicine ball, an elastic resistance band, or the athlete's own body weight.

Strength training for swimming does not focus on building large muscles. Big muscles are not necessarily strong muscles. In swimming, muscle size is not as important as muscle strength and flexibility, because large muscles can

...range of motion of joints. ... Michael Phelps's training ...ese attributes. "His shoul-...t about bulk, because he ... Wigo, former University ...chief executive officer of ...ll of Fame. "That comes ...g up and stretching. He'll ...hind his back to reach as ...lar across his shoulders as possible. He'll do this for fifteen minutes before a race."[8]

A strength-training workout for swimmers, as for any athlete, begins with a careful warm-up period, to warm the muscles, increase blood flow to the tissues, and improve the flexibility of the joints. The strength portion of the workout for swimmers focuses on exercises that mimic swimming movements and help make the athlete a better swimmer. It especially targets the muscles of the hips and legs, the core

A swimmer uses paddles during a practice lap to increase resistance as his hands move through the water. Swimmers use various forms of resistance training in and out of the pool in order to build muscle strength and power.

(the chest, abdomen, and back), and the arms and shoulders. For example, leg presses increase strength in the thighs and calves, for a better push off the starting block and a stronger kick in the water. The core muscles must be strong in several directions of movement in order to have the most effective arm stroke possible. Moving the trunk in several directions while holding a medicine ball is one of many ways swimmers can strengthen their core. After a workout, a period of careful stretching helps lengthen the muscles and increases joint and muscle flexibility, which improve performance and help the swimmer avoid injuries.

Putting Muscles to Work

The human body contains three major kinds of muscle tissue. Cardiac muscle makes up the heart. Smooth muscle makes up the walls of the hollow organs, such as the stomach, intestines, and bladder, and allows those organs to move substances, such as food and urine, through them. The muscle tissue involved in strength training is called skeletal muscle. Skeletal muscles allow humans to move all their body parts as they go through their daily activities. All movements, from running and jumping to smiling and frowning, depend on the action of skeletal muscle.

Skeletal muscles are very complex structures. They are made up of thousands of long fibers, or muscle cells, which run the length of the muscle from one end to the other. Groups of muscle fibers work with nerves called motor neurons, which allow the muscle to contract, or shorten, in length. Skeletal muscles are attached to the bones, usually at a joint, by tough, whitish bands called tendons. When a skeletal muscle contracts, it pulls on the tendon attached to the bone at the joint and moves the bone. For example, when a person wants to bend an elbow, the brain sends a signal to the motor neurons in the bicep muscle, located on the front of the upper arm. The signal tells the bicep to contract. When the bicep contracts, it pulls up on the tendons that attach it to the front side of the bones in the forearm. This pulls the forearm upward at the elbow. To straighten the arm, the tricep muscle, on the back of the upper arm, contracts and pulls on the tendons on the back side of the forearm bones, lowering the forearm back down.

When a person bends an elbow, the bicep does not have to work very hard to do it. If a person is holding a heavy weight in his or her hand, however, the weight creates resistance against the action of the bicep, so it must work much harder to raise the forearm plus the extra weight. When a muscle is made to work repetitively against heavy resistance, such as during a weight-lifting session, small microscopic tears happen in the muscle fibers. This micro-damage actually results in stronger muscles. Fitness expert Gabe Mirkin explains,

> Nobody really knows how these hard bouts make muscles stronger, but the most likely theory depends on the fact that hard exercise damages muscle fibers.... The damaged muscle cells release tissue growth factors to heal the damaged muscle fibers, and if the athlete allows the muscle soreness to disappear before exercising intensely again, muscle fibers become larger and increase in number by splitting to form new fibers.[9]

It is very important for the athlete to allow enough rest time between intense workouts for this healing process to take place. Low-intensity workouts done while the muscle is healing may be beneficial, however. Mirkin says, "If the athlete exercises at low intensity during recovery, his muscles will become more fibrous and resistant to injury when he stresses his muscles with the next intense bout of exercise."[10]

Training Day for Michael Phelps

Michael Phelps has been called one of the greatest athletes of all time. After winning a record-breaking eight gold medals at the 2008 Beijing Summer Olympics, a lot of people became interested in how he trains for competition.

Much has been made of Phelps's diet. An average man his age consumes about two thousand calories a day. Phelps typically takes in about twelve thousand calories each day, mostly carbohydrates. His breakfast alone usually consists of two fried egg sandwiches with cheese, lettuce, tomato, fried onions, and mayonnaise; three chocolate chip pancakes; an omelet; toast; three pieces of French toast with sugar; a bowl of grits; and oatmeal. Lunch and dinner include lots of pasta, pizza, sandwiches, and energy drinks. He also takes protein supplements.

All those calories get used, however, and Phelps maintains about 8 percent body fat. He trains six days a week without fail, including strength training in the gym three days a week, designed to maximize muscle endurance, stroke power, and flexibility. Aerobic conditioning is done mostly on a stationary bike. He also spends four to six hours a day in the pool, swimming the equivalent of about 8 miles (13km) each day. Ice baths and two massages a day help his muscles recover. His heart pumps about double the average amount of blood each minute, and his lactic acid production has been measured at about one-third the average swimmer's, allowing him to swim strong longer than other swimmers.

Developing Power

Along with strength, a swimmer needs to have muscle power. Power is related to strength, but it is not the same thing. Even a very strong athlete may lack power. Power combines strength with speed of motion. It means not only moving a weight, but also moving it quickly. For example, swimmers need power to get a good start off the starting block and to make strong, quick turns at the end of a lap.

The concept of power can be measured with a mathematical equation called the Force-Velocity Relationship:

$$\text{Power} = \text{Force} \times \frac{\text{Distance}}{\text{Time}}$$

In this equation, force is the amount of effort used to move the weight. Distance is how far the weight is being moved, and time is the length of time it takes the athlete to move the weight over the distance. Strength training improves power by increasing the "force" part of the equation. With more strength, the "time" part can be decreased. This means that the athlete can move weight through a particular distance in less time, which means more power.

Like training for strength, training for power also involves moving weight, but the weight is generally lighter so that the athlete can move it faster. Power training also differs from strength training in how the weight is moved. In strength training, energy is used to lift the weight up and also to control and then stop the weight on the way back down. In

Swimmers dive into the pool at the beginning of a race. Training for power, which focuses on the speed at which muscles can move a weight, helps swimmers improve off the starting block and at turns at the end of a lap.

power training, weights are moved in such a way that the athlete does not have to stop the weight. An example of this is using a medicine ball. The athlete must apply a lot of force to throw the heavy ball, but the athlete does not have to use any energy to stop it because it leaves the hands at the end of the movement. This kind of movement develops power in the muscles of the front and sides of the chest, important for strokes such as the front crawl and the butterfly. Olympic champion Michael Phelps uses a medicine ball as part of his gym workout to strengthen his core muscles. Another example of a power exercise swimmers use is the squat jump, in which the swimmer holds a barbell across his or her shoulders, squats down, then pushes up quickly enough to leave the floor briefly. This develops power in the legs for pushing off the starting block and making strong turns off the wall.

Endurance

Endurance is the ability to repeat a muscle movement many times in a row without fatigue. Endurance is important in swimming, especially long distance swimming, because fatigue decreases speed and interferes with proper mechanics. Endurance depends not only on muscle strength but also on the body's ability to supply the muscles with a steady supply of oxygen, essential for healthy cell function, and on its ability to tap into other sources of energy when the oxygen supply is depleted. Endurance requires excellent cardiovascular fitness—healthy lungs to draw in the oxygen and get it into the blood, a healthy heart to pump the blood, and healthy blood vessels to carry the oxygen to all the body's cells.

Like all cells in any living organism, when muscle cells are working, chemical reactions take place inside the cell. The process of chemical reactions that let a cell carry out its function is called metabolism. Metabolism is an extremely complex process, involving over two dozen separate chemical reactions, but it is basically similar to the way a car uses gasoline as fuel. The body's cells use sugar, or glucose, as the fuel, with oxygen necessary to drive the process. This is called aerobic (with oxygen) metabolism. Just as a car produces waste products in the form of exhaust, cell metabolism

An athlete undergoes a VO2 max test to measure his oxygen consumption during exercise. This provides a measure of his aerobic fitness, which is critical to success in competitive swimming.

produces waste products as well. The waste products of aerobic cell metabolism are carbon dioxide and water, which are removed from the body by breathing. As a person increases exercise intensity, he or she must breathe faster and harder in order to get the necessary oxygen into the blood.

Aerobic endurance is the efficiency with which the body, by breathing, can deliver oxygen to the muscles and remove the waste products created by muscle metabolism. Aerobic endurance can be measured with a test called a maximal oxygen uptake test, also called the VO2 max. *V* stands for "volume" and "O2" refers to oxygen. The VO2 max measures oxygen consumption—the athlete's maximum ability to use

Doping in Swimming

In the early 1980s, Birgit Meineke of the German Democratic Republic was the fastest freestyle swimmer in the world. As a star athlete in East Germany, she received the best medical care her country could provide, including, starting at age twelve and unknown to her, daily doses of drugs called anabolic steroids.

Anabolic steroids are man-made chemicals that mimic the effects of male hormones, such as testosterone. They stimulate protein synthesis, especially in muscle tissue, which leads to the rapid buildup of muscle. They also lead to the development of masculine characteristics, such as aggressive behavior, thickening of the vocal cords, and growth of body hair. Athletes in many sports have used steroids to give themselves a competitive edge and to help them heal injuries more quickly. Since the 1980s, the meteoric rise in financial rewards of athletic success has increased the temptation to use these drugs.

The abuse of anabolic steroids has many potentially dangerous effects as well. By the time Meineke was fifteen years old, people had started to notice that her voice was deepening. She suffered severe outbreaks of acne. In 1993, she was diagnosed with hepatitis, a liver disease, and with a tumor in her liver, which are known to be associated with the abuse of steroids. For these reasons, the use of "performance enhancing" steroids and stimulant drugs, called doping, is now illegal in most sports, including competitive swimming. Athletes are routinely tested for such drugs before competition. Those who test positive risk disqualification and the loss of medals already won.

oxygen for cell metabolism. It is considered to be the best measure of an athlete's aerobic fitness. VO2 max is measured by having the athlete exercise on a cycle or a treadmill. As the intensity of the exercise is increased, the amounts of oxygen being inhaled and exhaled are measured. This indicates how much oxygen the athlete is using. VO2 max is reached when oxygen consumption remains steady even when exercise intensity is increased.

Competitive swimming requires enough stamina and endurance to swim hard for an extended period of time. Serious competitive swimmers have their VO2 max measured as an indication of their aerobic endurance. It is very difficult to take such measurements while the swimmer is actually swimming, but it can be measured somewhat accurately while exercising on a stationary bike or treadmill. Another test used to measure a swimmer's endurance is called the Critical Swim Speed test. In this test, the swimmer is timed swimming 437 yards (400m) and then 55 yards (50m), as fast as he or she can, with a ten-minute rest between swims. A calculation is done using the two times to determine the Critical Swim Speed.

Anaerobic Metabolism

Stronger muscles use oxygen more efficiently than weaker ones, so a strong athlete can exercise longer and more effectively than a weaker one. However, if an athlete exercises so hard that he or she cannot get enough oxygen into the blood for aerobic metabolism, the person has reached what is called the metabolic threshold, and the muscles begin to produce a different waste product called lactate. This is called anaerobic (without oxygen) metabolism. When lactate begins to accumulate in the blood faster than the body can get rid of it, the athlete has reached what is called the lactate threshold.

Anaerobic metabolism with lactate accumulation leads to fatigue, discomfort, and weakened muscles. Eventually the person has to slow down and rest in order to replenish the oxygen level. As the person recovers, the lactate which has accumulated can be converted into glucose and used as an energy source but only for a few minutes. Lactate can also be converted to carbon dioxide and water and eliminated through the lungs.

Training for Endurance

Swimmers train to increase their endurance by improving both their aerobic and anaerobic fitness. Common endurance training methods include distance swimming, cycling, or running. There are several levels of endurance training

In order to perform to the best of their ability, swimmers must be conscious of how they breathe and how breathing affects their endurance and speed as they move through the water. Inhalation and exhalation involve a number of muscles, including the intercostal muscles and the diaphragm, which separates the chest and the abdomen.

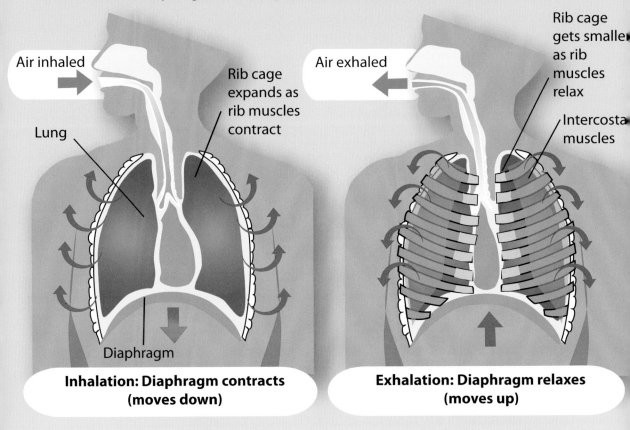

Air inhaled

Rib cage expands as rib muscles contract

Lung

Diaphragm

Inhalation: Diaphragm contracts (moves down)

Air exhaled

Rib cage gets smaller as rib muscles relax

Intercostal muscles

Exhalation: Diaphragm relaxes (moves up)

in which a swimmer may participate, depending on how intensely the exercise is done. Base endurance training involves low to moderate intensity periods of the exercise, which enhance the ability of the muscles to use oxygen efficiently. Aerobic maintenance increases the intensity to further work the heart and lungs. Threshold endurance training sessions increase the intensity but shorten the length of the session. Threshold work brings the swimmer close to his lactate threshold. Overload endurance training is high-intensity training, which pushes the muscles past what they are used to, increasing their strength and endurance. Anaerobic training includes short, fast, high-intensity sprints and longer, very high-intensity sessions with rest periods long enough to eliminate lactate. It trains the body to endure past the lactate threshold.

STARTING BLOCK

80 inches

Michael Phelps's "wing span," the distance from fingertip to fingertip, which is about 4 inches longer than his height.

A study conducted by the University of Buffalo in New York and published in 2006 shows that swimmers and underwater divers can improve their endurance, and therefore their performance, by specifically training the muscles that are used for breathing. "Typically, we think it's the muscles that move the body that are fatigued when we tire," says Claes Lundgren, professor of physiology at the university and lead author of the study. "However, the increased work load of the breathing muscles is very important, particularly underwater during prolonged or high intensity exercise such as swimming. Increasing the strength and endurance of the respiratory muscles prevents their fatigue during sustained exercise, enabling divers and swimmers to sustain their effort longer without tiring."[11] Swimmers can train their breathing muscles by breathing against a resistance, such as a valve under pressure, or by doing sessions of faster, deeper breathing.

Proper breathing techniques are critical for competitive swimmers in order to get the maximum amount of oxygen into the body and maximize endurance. Swimmers spend a great deal of training time just learning how to breathe properly while swimming. Breathing skills that swimmers practice may include exhaling under water so that there is more time to inhale while the head is above water, keeping the head still when not breathing, not lifting the head forward to breathe (which can cause the legs to sink), and being able to breathe with the head turned either to the right or the left, instead of just one direction. Developing a good body roll while doing the front crawl helps get the head turned out of the water without straining the neck. Another technique is diaphragmatic breathing: breathing in using the abdominal muscles rather than the chest muscles. Many coaches feel that diaphragmatic breathing allows deeper breaths than chest breathing.

Improving Speed

One of the most significant differences between swimming and other sports is that it is the only sport that is done in the water. Water has been described as being as much as a thousand times denser than air. This means that it is much more difficult to move quickly through water than through air. Elite cyclists can travel as fast as 37 miles per hour (60kmh). Top runners can hit speeds of up to 25 miles per hour (40kmh) at the end of a sprint. Swimmers, however, rarely break 5 miles per hour (8kmh) because of the density of water.

Training for speed in swimming once concentrated mostly on endurance training. Today, science and technology play a much larger role in developing training programs for swimming speed. According to Genadijus Sokolovas, former director of physiology and sport science for USA Swimming, the governing body for swimming in the United States, swimmers now spend as much as 50 percent of their training on improving technical aspects of their sport. Video

Olympic champion Michael Phelps's left hand enters the water bent at a 45-degree angle, which allows him to maximize the speed of each arm stroke.

of the swimmer in the water is commonly used to closely examine a swimmer's technique, including the take off, the stroke, the kick, the turn, and alignment of the body in the water. These techniques are examined from above and below the water and from several different angles. Computers create digital images of the swimmer, which are also used to closely analyze the technique of the swimmer's strokes.

Technology such as this has helped swimming champions such as Michael Phelps adapt their strokes for maximum speed. "He uses his hands like a sculler [a person using oars to propel a boat] uses the tips of his oars–he has a terrific technique," says Wigo. "Many swimmers press their hands down on the water flat. Michael doesn't. His hands hit the water at a precise 45-degree angle. This has the effect of better gripping the water and 'pulling it back' to increase velocity."[12] Advanced testing equipment operated by trained exercise physiologists measures a swimmer's VO2 and lactate levels as he exercises. Swimmers at the 2008 Summer Olympics were accompanied by four sports science experts, who analyzed film of each race and tested each athlete's lactate levels immediately after each race.

All these scientific and technological advances in training are geared toward increasing the swimmers' speed and maximizing his or her chances of succeeding in competition. Since 2000, dozens of world records have been broken as a result of advanced technology and sports science. "You probably can't stop technology from coming into any sport," says Sokolovas. "If athletes want to swim faster, technology will always be there. I don't see it as bad. It's good for the popularity of swimming. It gets more people interested in sport. And what is the goal of sport? A healthier nation."[13]

Nutrition for Swimmers

Swimming is a sport which requires a great deal of energy, strength, and endurance. These qualities can only be developed if the swimmer provides his or her body with plenty of good quality fuel by eating a healthy diet geared toward the needs of a swimmer. Training is useless without the nutrients necessary for cell metabolism and growth.

Nutrients are the chemicals in food that provide the body with the necessary fuel for optimum function of all its cells. They provide energy in the form of calories. A calorie is a way to measure energy, like a mile measures distance or a pound measures weight. Calories are necessary even during sleep, because energy is needed to fuel the body's functions that keep it alive, such as breathing, heartbeat, digestion, growth, and many other functions people do not often think about. A person who exercises a lot needs to consume a lot of calories. Swimmers need a lot of calories to satisfy their energy requirements. The three types of calorie-producing nutrients contained in a balanced, healthy diet are carbohydrates, fats, and protein.

Carbohydrates

Carbohydrates (commonly called "carbs") come in two forms, simple and complex. Simple carbohydrates are sugars. They are digested quickly in the body and provide short bursts of energy. Simple carbs are found in foods such as white sugar, fruits, dairy products, pasta, white rice, and white bread. Complex carbohydrates take longer to digest but provide longer-lasting energy. They are found in foods such as whole-grain breads and pastas, oatmeal, vegetables, brown rice, and beans. One gram (about a third of an ounce) of carbohydrate provides four calories of energy.

Carbohydrates are the body's preferred first source of energy. When a person eats a carbohydrate, the liver breaks it down into a simple sugar called glucose, which is used as fuel by many types of cells. Any excess glucose gets stored in the liver and the muscles in the form of a chemical called glycogen. If the body needs extra calories for any reason, it converts its glycogen stores back into glucose. Basic nutritional guidelines recommend that about 60 percent of a person's daily calories should come from carbohydrates. A large percentage of a swimmer's diet consists of carbs, especially complex carbs, and the basic percentage may be increased to 70 percent or more for several days before competing.

Fats

If a person exercises for a long period of time and uses up the body's carbohydrates and stores of glycogen, the body will turn to fats, also called lipids, as a fuel source. A gram of fat provides nine calories of energy. Fat also provides insulation to keep the internal organs warm and protected, especially important for open-water swimmers, and helps the body use other nutrients as well as certain vitamins and minerals. Fats can be found in both animal and plant food sources. Animal fats are found in dairy products, such as butter and cream, poultry skin, and fat attached to meat. Plant fats are usually oils, such as peanut oil, corn oil, and olive oil.

Protein

Protein is a critical part of a swimmer's diet for many reasons. Every structure of the body and every cell function require some kind of protein. Hair, fingernails, and the lens of the eye are made of pure protein. Proteins help digestion and allow muscles to grow, to repair themselves after exercise, and to move. Some hormones, such as insulin necessary for sugar metabolism, are proteins. Antibodies, which fight disease-causing organisms, are proteins. The protein hemoglobin is what carries oxygen in the blood, necessary to the swimmer for good endurance. Even the genetic material which makes people human, their DNA, is made of protein.

Protein is absolutely essential for all organisms to live. For this reason, very little of it is ever used as fuel as long as carbohydrate and fat stores are adequate. It is the last resort for the body as a source of fuel, used only when carbohydrates and fat have been completely consumed. A person forced to use protein for calories will gradually waste away—a condition called cachexia (ka-KEX-ia)—and will eventually die.

Water, Vitamins, and Minerals

Water, vitamins, and minerals are not considered nutrients, because they do not provide calories for energy. They are, however, essential for optimum cell function and, therefore, essential for optimum athletic performance.

Water is an essential component of cell metabolism, as well as being a by-product of metabolism. Water allows essential chemicals to pass into and out of the cells and keeps these chemicals in their proper balance. It provides lubrication for all the body's moving parts. It serves as a way to transport substances through the bloodstream. It helps maintain healthy body temperature. Inadequate water intake leads to a condition called dehydration, which interferes with both physical and mental performance.

Vitamins are organic (found in living organisms) compounds that have many varied functions in the body. There are thirteen known vitamins. Some regulate mineral metabolism, such as vitamin D, which is necessary for the body to use the mineral calcium. Others, such as vitamin A, regulate cell growth. The B vitamins play a role in cell metabolism and in the use of carbohydrates, proteins, and fats. Most vitamins cannot be produced in the body, so they must be taken in with food. A balanced diet helps to ensure that a person is consuming all the vitamins needed for good health.

Minerals are nonorganic, chemical elements which are also required by living organisms. Examples of some

A balanced diet that emphasizes complex carbohydrates, fruits and vegetables, lean proteins, and a range of vitamins and minerals will provide swimmers with a competitive edge.

important elements are calcium, potassium, iron, and sodium. Minerals are needed for both structure and function of the cells. For example, calcium is necessary for the building and maintenance of strong bones, muscles, teeth, and nerves. Dairy products are the best source of calcium. Iron is essential for the blood to carry oxygen. It is found in meats, beans, and dark-green leafy vegetables, such spinach. Sodium has a very important role in fluid balance and kidney function. Sodium is found in salty foods, such as salted crackers and nuts, canned soups, and tomato sauce.

Carbohydrates, proteins, fats, water, vitamins, and minerals are all very important to a swimmer. Without them, the body's cells cannot function optimally, training and conditioning are ineffective, and the swimmer will not perform to the best of his or her ability. At the same time, the swimmer must avoid taking other substances which can be very harmful, such as caffeine, which can cause dehydration; cigarette smoke, which damages the heart and lungs and can cause cancer; alcohol, which damages the liver, interferes with nutrients, and impairs mental sharpness; and steroid supplements, which can cause a host of very severe, long-term health problems.

CHAPTER 3

Injuries and Hazards

S wimming is considered a low-impact type of exercise, because except for on-land training, there is little to no weight-bearing impact on the joints, bones, and muscles. It is also a noncontact sport in that, with the possible exception of water polo, there is little or no physical contact between competitors. There is no hard ground to come in contact with, and (also with the exception of water polo) no thrown or batted equipment to strike swimmers. It might seem that swimmers have very little chance to get hurt, but there are certain injuries to which swimmers are prone. Most are caused by overtraining or by long-term, repetitive movement against the resistance of the water. There are also certain hazards uniquely related to swimming.

Swimming Injuries

All sports injuries are described as either acute injuries or overuse injuries. Acute injuries are those that happen suddenly, without any warning, and are often the result of accidents, such as slipping on a wet poolside. Acute injuries are rare in swimming, especially in competitive swimming, in which the participants are well trained. When they do occur, they are usually minor and interfere very little with the swimmer's ability to perform. A swimmer may jam a

A swimmer gets her neck massaged during a training session. Neck, shoulder, back, and knee injuries can occur with swimmers because of the strains of repetitive motion and overuse on joints and muscles.

finger against the side of the pool or strain a muscle during weight training. Allowing the injured part to rest until pain is gone and applying a cold pack to minimize swelling is usually sufficient treatment for these minor types of injuries.

Most injuries to swimmers, however, are overuse injuries. These are injuries that result from long-term, repetitive use

STARTING BLOCK

7

The number of bones in the neck in both humans and giraffes.

of a joint or muscle. They are caused by microscopic damage to the tissues which, if not allowed to heal completely, builds up over time. Because the upper body is responsible for most of the work in swimming, the most common overuse injuries occur in the neck, shoulder, and back. Overuse injuries can also occur in the hips, knees, and groin area as well.

Neck Pain in Swimming

The neck is a very complex part of the body. It is supported by the bones of the neck, called the cervical spine. There are seven bones, or vertebrae, in the cervical spine. The cervical vertebrae are separated from each other and cushioned by spongy layers called intervertebral discs, which allow flexibility in the neck and act as shock absorbers. The delicate spinal cord, which carries messages in the form of nerve impulses from the brain to the rest of the body, runs through the vertebrae from the base of the brain to the lower back. Along the way, spinal nerves come off the spinal cord, pass between the vertebrae, and carry the nerve impulses to the muscles, joints, and skin, allowing body parts to move and to feel sensations, such as heat, cold, and pain. The neck also contains many small muscles, which allow it to move in many different directions, and several larger muscles, which span the neck and the upper back. Also in the neck are several important blood vessels, which carry blood to and from the head. Other important structures in the neck include the trachea, or windpipe; the larynx, or voice box; and the esophagus, or food tube to the stomach.

Neck pain in swimmers is usually caused by muscle strain because of poor body alignment in the water. For example, while doing the front crawl, a swimmer may hold the head in a slightly face-forward position when swimming, instead of facing straight down toward the bottom of the pool. This strains the back of the neck. In the backstroke, the muscles on the front of the neck may be strained from trying to keep the head facing up or from flexing the neck too far forward.

A COMPLEX STRUCTURE

As swimmers train and compete, they learn techniques to avoid damaging areas vulnerable to injury, such as the neck. The human neck is composed of a number of key structures, including the spinal cord, which carries nerve impulses to the entire body.

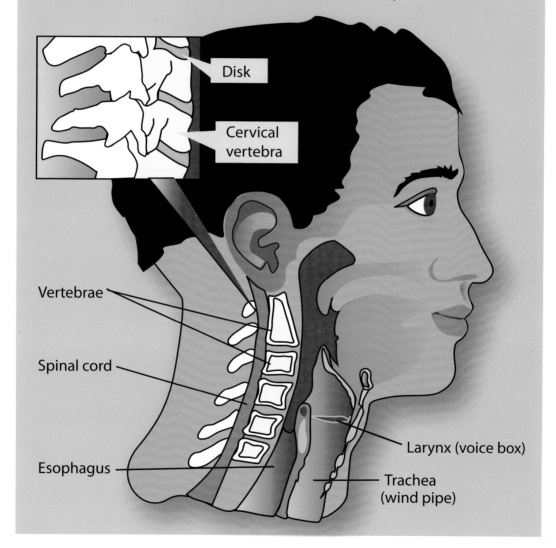

Disk

Cervical vertebra

Vertebrae

Spinal cord

Esophagus

Larynx (voice box)

Trachea (wind pipe)

Faulty breathing mechanics are often responsible for misalignment of the neck. A swimmer may tend to lift the head forward or upward when taking a breath instead of simply turning the head to the side. Others may tuck the chin down toward their shoulder when breathing, or they may turn the neck too far when taking a breath. In the breaststroke, the swimmer may tilt the head too far back when coming up for a breath. In the butterfly, neck muscles may be strained if the swimmer does not get enough height out of the water to breathe correctly.

Problems with body alignment causing neck pain can be spotted by closely examining and correcting the swimmer's stroke mechanics. Treatment for neck strain varies. Jessica Seaton, a chiropractor and swimmer says,

> Depending on the practitioner, treatment will vary. Chiropractors and osteopaths will manipulate the joints of the neck in appropriate cases. Physical therapists and chiropractors may use non-force techniques such as mobilization (gently stretching your neck in different directions), muscle energy techniques, ultrasound, electrical current, and specific stretching exercises. If the problem is mainly in the muscles, massage by a qualified massage therapist may help.[14]

Swimmer's Shoulder

All swimming strokes require constant, repetitive use of the arms and shoulders to provide most of the power for movement through the water. When combined with strength training in the gym, this constant use of the shoulder joint against resistance causes microscopic damage to the tissues of the joint, especially if the stroke technique is faulty or if the swimmer overtrains. Over time, this microdamage leads to a painful overuse condition known as swimmer's shoulder. Swimmer's shoulder is the most common of the overuse injuries in swimmers, affecting as many as 75 percent of competitive swimmers.

Like the neck, the shoulder is very complex, containing several bones and joints, muscles and tendons, nerves, and blood vessels. Altogether, this area is known as the shoulder girdle. The shoulder can move in more different directions than any other joint in the body–forward and backward, up

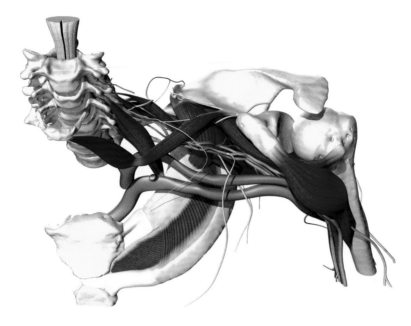

The structure of the human shoulder girdle contains several bones and joints, muscles, tendons, nerves, and blood vessels. Swimmers are susceptible to injuries that can affect any of these components.

and down, across the body and away from it, and around in circles. The three main bones of the shoulder are the humerus, or upper arm bone; the scapula, or shoulder blade; and the clavicle, or collar bone. These three bones come together in the shoulder to form two joints. The glenohumeral joint is where the ball of the humerus fits into the glenoid, a small cup, or socket, in the scapula. The acromioclavicular joint is between the clavicle and the acromion, the front part of the scapula. A third joint that may cause trouble in the shoulder area is the sternoclavicular joint, where the clavicle meets the sternum, or breastbone, in the center of the chest. These joints are kept stable by ligaments, bands of tough tissue which support the joints and keep the bones aligned properly with each other. Several muscles also contribute to the strength and stability of the shoulder joint, in particular, four small muscles which together with their tendons are called the rotator cuff. The rotator cuff muscles help raise the arm to the side and rotate the shoulder in its many directions. They also help keep the humerus from popping out of the glenoid.

Also running through the shoulder joint are important nerves and blood vessels. The nerves carry messages from the brain to the rest of the arm, allowing the arm to move and to feel pain, touch, and temperature. Large blood vessels carry fresh, oxygen-rich blood to the tissues of the arm and return deoxygenated blood to the heart to be pumped to the lungs.

Most commonly, swimmer's shoulder is caused by one or a combination of three problems: inflammation, impingement, or instability. Inflammation is a normal response by the body to any kind of irritation or damage. It occurs when tissues in the shoulder, especially tendons (a condition called tendonitis), are repeatedly irritated and damaged from overuse and not allowed enough time to heal. It also results from more severe damage in the shoulder, such as a tear in the rotator cuff muscles. Symptoms of inflammation include swelling, pain, and loss of some joint function. If not treated, inflammation can lead to the buildup of scar tissue in the joint, a process called fibrosis, which can result in permanent loss of function.

Impingement happens when soft tissues, such as rotator cuff muscles, become trapped between the acromion of the scapula and the humerus. It is especially common in sports that require frequent overhead movement of the arms, such as in swimming, baseball, and tennis. It can happen because of inflammation and swelling of the joint tissues or occasionally because of a torn rotator cuff muscle. When a muscle is impinged, its blood circulation is decreased, and the muscle becomes fragile and more prone to tearing. Impingement causes pain when the arm is lifted overhead or up behind the back.

Instability of the shoulder occurs when the rotator cuff muscles and tendons become loose and do not hold the humerus securely in its socket. The shoulder is especially prone to instability because of the many directions in which it moves. Instability may cause abnormal or excessive movement of the humerus in the joint, or it may cause the humerus to come completely out of its socket, called dislocation of the shoulder. Shoulder instability can be caused by previous injury to the rotator cuff, or it can result from a natural laxity, or looseness, of the rotator cuff. It can also be caused by unbalanced strength training, which causes part of the rotator cuff to be weaker than the rest of it.

Treatment for swimmer's shoulder includes rest until pain is gone, longer warm-up sessions, icing the shoulder after workouts, physical therapy, and anti-inflammatory medications for pain and swelling. More severe problems, such as rotator cuff tears and repeated shoulder dislocations, may require surgery. Close analysis of the swimmer's stroke, careful strength training for the rotator cuff, and gentle stretching of the shoulder, neck, and chest muscles can help prevent shoulder problems from occurring.

Back Pain

According to back pain expert Bianca Diaz, "in many cases, swimming can be a very helpful exercise for back pain sufferers. Athletes commonly become injured, and swimming is a great way to keep active since it does not put excess strain on a swimmer's back. However, that's not to say that swimming can't cause back pain or injuries as well."[15] This is especially true if improper stroke techniques are used. Strokes such as the breaststroke and butterfly, with their rapid up-and-down movements, are particularly prone to causing back pain if done improperly. The dolphin-style kick of the butterfly also creates problems for the lower back if done improperly. Problems arise if the swimmer allows the natural curve in the lower back to become exaggerated like a swaybacked horse, a posture called hyperextension or lordosis. When this happens in the water, the muscles of the lower back must work harder to keep the lower body afloat, a job better done by the core muscles of the chest and abdomen. Lordosis causes lower back pain, because it strains the lower back muscles and their ligaments, and because it causes the joints between the vertebrae in the back, called facets, to press abnormally on each other. Over time, the excess stress on the lower vertebrae can actually cause small fractures in the bones called stress fractures.

Back pain after swimming can be treated with rest, ice, gentle stretching, and anti-inflammatory medications. More persistent pain may require physical therapy or the temporary use of a back brace. Swimmers can help prevent back

X-ray images compare a spine with lordosis, left, with a healthy spine. Lordosis is an exaggerated curve of the spine that can result when certain swimming strokes and kicks are done improperly, thus straining the back and causing pain.

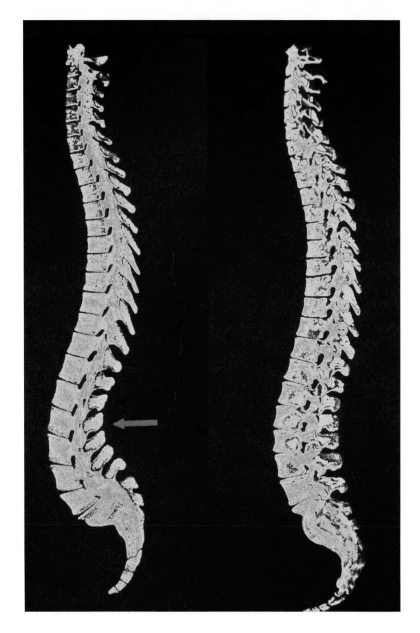

pain by observing good body mechanics in the water, not allowing the lower back to become hyperextended, and by doing careful strength training exercises designed for the back muscles. Diaz says,

> If swimming continues to be painful, it's important to stop and seek that advice of a physician in order to stop back pain. By continuing to swim despite continual or

worsening pain, the condition affecting the back may become worse and more serious forms of treatment may be required to reverse discomfort. Only in rare cases is surgery required to reverse ailments that affect the back. However, there are still instances where surgery may not be enough to completely reverse back pain conditions.[16]

Breaststroker's Knee

The knee is a hinge-type joint that is designed to move primarily in one direction, that is, to move the lower leg forward and backward. The knee is not designed for much side-to-side movement. The whip kick of the breaststroke, however, requires the legs to move in a sideways direction as the knees are bent and the legs are separated, turned outward, then quickly extended and brought back together. This sideways force, especially during the extension part of the kick, puts a lot of stress on the ligaments in the knee that provide the knee with stability from side to side. Breaststroker's knee is caused by repeated strain on the medial collateral ligament, the ligament on the inside, or medial side, of the knee. The main symptom is pain on the inside of the knee.

Another consequence of repeated sideways stress on the knee is instability of the kneecap, or patella, from stress on the ligament that holds it at the center of the knee. This can cause the patella to move too far toward the outside of the knee. If the patella becomes too unstable, inflammation and pain result, and surgery may be required to restabilize the patella at the center of the knee.

Breaststroker's knee is treated similarly to other swimming injuries, with rest, ice, pain medication, longer warm-up periods, physical therapy, and strengthening exercises for the muscles of the thigh. Swimmers, especially those who use the breaststroke frequently, are often encouraged by their doctors to take two months off from the stroke each year to allow the medial collateral ligament to heal. As with other swimming injuries, careful attention to the swimmer's kick technique helps prevent breaststroker's knee.

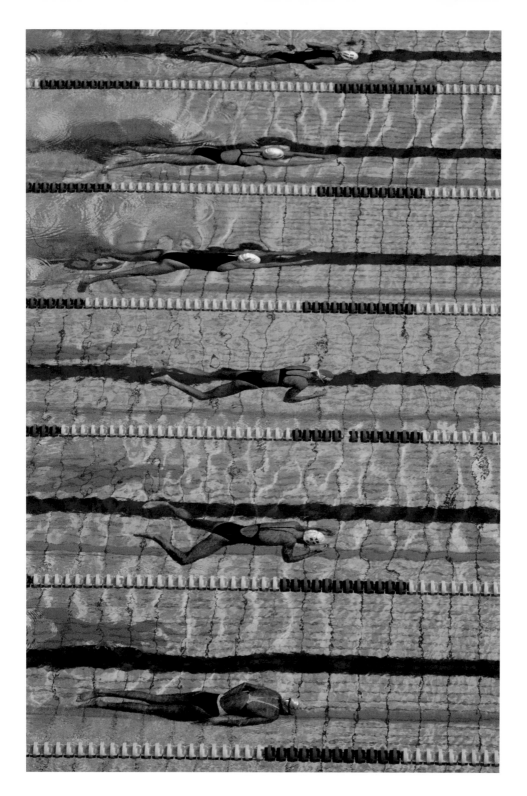

Acclimating to Cold Water

It is possible for open-water swimmers to temporarily acclimate, or adapt themselves, to cold water before an open-water race or event, which allows them to tolerate lower temperatures for longer periods of time and helps prevent or lessen hypothermia. One way to do this is to swim in cold water for twenty to thirty minutes several times a week for the three to four weeks before the event in which they plan to participate. Another way is to take cold baths, including adding ice to the bath water, several times a week. Over time, the heart and lungs adapt to the cold by decreasing their response to "cold shock," which includes a sudden increase in heart rate and blood pressure, involuntary gasping, and rapid breathing.

Swimmers race in an open water competition, where conditions are typically challenging. Their training regimen includes techniques that help their bodies tolerate cold water temperatures while performing at their best.

Swimmers can also help avoid the effects of hypothermia by wearing an insulating wetsuit to prevent heat loss from conduction and by eating a high-carbohydrate meal (which increases glucose levels) before an event so glycogen stores will not be depleted as quickly.

Hazards of Swimming

Swimming has certain dangers and hazards associated with it which are not present in other sports. Open-water swimmers and divers are especially vulnerable to these hazards,

Swimmers in an Olympic race show the varied leg positions of the breaststroke's kicking motion, which pushes the legs out sideways from the body with the knees bent before they are brought straight together.

An exhausted open-water swimmer is carried from the ocean after winning a race in rough, cold conditions. Such competitions often present many dangers to swimmers.

as are young or inexperienced swimmers, or swimmers who are under the influence of drugs or alcohol.

Swimmers who participate in long-distance endurance swimming face their own set of potential hazards associated with open-water swimming. Endurance swimmers are vulnerable to seasickness, exhaustion, and muscle cramping, and there are no pool sides to hold on to in open water. Currents and wind conditions can sweep swimmers far off their course. Hazards under the water include sharp objects, such as rocks or tree branches; seaweed; and stings or bites from potentially dangerous aquatic wildlife.

Open bodies of water are usually colder than swimming pools. Prolonged immersion in cold water can significantly lower the internal, or core, body temperature, a condition called hypothermia. Hypothermia is a very common, and potentially very dangerous, hazard of open-water swimming.

Hypothermia

Hypothermia is an abnormally low core body temperature that is caused by prolonged exposure to cold conditions. Normal body temperature ranges from about 95 °F (35 °C) to about 100 °F (38 °C), depending on time of day and in what part of the body the temperature is taken. Hypothermia is defined as a core temperature lower than 94 °F (34 °C). Open-water swimmers risk hypothermia when they spend hours in cold water, especially if there is also a cold wind or if they have little body fat to serve as insulation.

When immersed in cold water, the body can lose as much as twenty to thirty times more heat than on land. This is because cold water draws heat out of the body through a process called conduction, in which heat is transferred from one molecule to another through a liquid, in this case, cold water. Heat loss is also increased if the water is moving quickly around the person, as it does in open-water swimming, a process called convection. In water that is at 50 °F (10 °C), severe hypothermia can occur in less than one hour.

Hypothermia can be a life-threatening condition. Early signs of hypothermia include uncontrolled shivering, pale skin, numbness in the hands and feet, and sleepiness. Shivering is the body's way of trying to generate more heat through rapid muscle contraction. This quickly uses up the swimmer's supply of glycogen, a chemical made in the liver that serves as a secondary source of energy after glucose. For this reason, fatigue and weakness may set in more quickly in cold water. Signs of severe hypothermia may include mental disturbances, confusion, loss of concern for safety, and clumsy movements. A swimmer who becomes severely hypothermic is in danger of becoming disoriented and is in danger of drowning. At a body temperature of about 90 °F (32 °C), shivering stops, and the swimmer is likely to lose consciousness. Hypothermia can cause the heart to slow down and become ineffective at pumping blood, and at about 86 °F (30 °C), cardiac

LOSING HEAT THROUGH CONDUCTION AND CONVECTION

Warm molecules move faster and hold more energy than cold molecules, and can transfer their heat through direct contact. While in wat[er] a swimmer will lose body heat to the surround ing water through this process, which is called **conduction**. In moving water, heat loss is inter sified because water warmed by the body is continuously being replaced by cold water, an[d] the new cold water is constantly taking heat from the body. This process is called **convectio**[n]

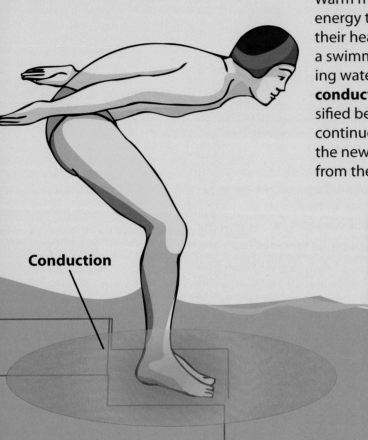

Conduction

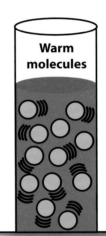

Warm molecules

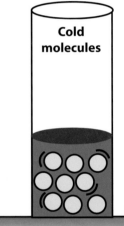

Cold molecules

Convection

arrest (complete stoppage of the heart) is likely. In water that is near freezing, death from hypothermia can occur within minutes.

Drowning

Drowning is a catastrophic event in which the lungs fill with fluid and cannot deliver adequate amounts of oxygen to the blood and, consequently, to the cells of the body, a condition called hypoxia. Drowning is a potential hazard for any swimmer, of any age or skill level. It can and often does lead to permanent brain damage or death. In the United States, drowning is the second-leading cause of death (after motor vehicle accidents) for children under twelve years of age and is the leading cause of death for children ages two to five. Males drown at a rate three times higher than females, usually because of reckless behavior or alcohol use. Among elite swimmers, it is extremely rare, although it is a particular hazard for open-water swimmers, who are vulnerable to exhaustion or hypothermia.

A conscious person who is immersed in water and cannot get his or her head above the surface will try to hold their breath for as long as possible. Eventually, however, the breathing reflex will cause the person to inhale, even under water. The process of drowning is very quick, with several events occurring within minutes. When water suddenly enters the lungs, the larynx, or vocal cords, closes involuntarily. This reflex, called laryngospasm, prevents both water and air from entering the lungs. The brain is especially vulnerable to hypoxia, and within two to three minutes, the person becomes unconscious. At this point, the laryngospasm relaxes, which allows more water to enter the lungs. At about the same time, cardiac arrest occurs, and the heart stops beating. After about six minutes without oxygen, brain damage or brain death occurs.

Contrary to common belief, drowning does not always result in death. If the drowning victim is removed from the water quickly, rescue measures may

STARTING BLOCK

40%
The percentage of drownings that happen on Saturdays and Sundays.

The Mammalian Dive Reflex

Drowning causes a lack of oxygen to vital organs, such as the brain, and can result in death in only a few minutes. An exception to this rule is sometimes seen in people who have been suddenly submerged into very cold water. Some people have survived up to an hour underwater without any apparent permanent physical damage. This phenomenon is known as the mammalian dive reflex and is commonly seen in diving mammals and birds, such as dolphins and penguins. Like other reflexes in humans, it is triggered by a sudden stimulus, in this case, the rapid immersion of the face and body into very cold water. It is not triggered by gradual immersion. Several physiological responses make this reflex possible. First, smaller blood vessels, such as those in the arms, hands, legs, and feet, constrict (vasoconstriction), decreasing blood flow to nonessential parts of the body. Second, as a result of vasoconstriction, more blood is shunted, or diverted, to the vital organs, especially the brain and heart. Third, as the body cools, its metabolic rate, and therefore its need for oxygen, decreases, and the heartbeat slows to a below-normal rate (bradycardia). The goal for rescuers is to get victims out of the water, get them warmed up, and get them on oxygen therapy before their available oxygen stores are used up. The mammalian dive reflex is most often seen in children and may gradually be lost with aging.

save the person's life even if he or she is not breathing and has no heartbeat. Cardiopulmonary resuscitation (CPR) can be started while the person is still in the water, with mouth-to-mouth rescue breathing. When medical professionals are present, a breathing tube can be inserted into the trachea and connected to a ventilator to support respiration. Medications are given to minimize lung inflammation and prevent further laryngospasm. Warming measures, such as increasing the room temperature, covering the person with a heating blanket, and giving warmed fluids into the veins help to counteract the effects of hypothermia.

Diving Injuries

At the 1988 Summer Olympics in Seoul, Korea, American diver Greg Louganis, considered by many swimming experts to be the best diver in the world, attempted a reverse two-and-a-half

somersault dive off the 10-foot (3m) springboard. He failed to get enough separation from the board, and on the way down, he hit his head sharply on the end of the board. He tumbled awkwardly into the water but was able to get out of the pool with help from medical personnel. Fortunately, he was not hurt badly, getting only a gash on the top of his head that needed a few stitches. "I didn't realize I was that close to the board," Louganis said later. "When I hit it, it was kind of a shock. But I think my pride was hurt more than anything else."[17] Louganis returned to the pool that day, finished his dives, and went on to win the gold medal in the springboard event.

It was not the first time Louganis had hit his head while diving. At a competition in 1979, he hit his head against a concrete diving platform. He was unconscious when he hit the water and remained so for about twenty minutes. He was lucky: He made a full recovery. Russian diver Sergei Chalibashvili was not so lucky. At the 1983 World University Games in Canada, he also hit his head against the concrete platform from which he was attempting a reverse three-and-a-half somersault dive. After a week in a coma, Chalibashvili died from his injury.

Injuries that occur during springboard or platform diving usually involve injuries to the head, face, or neck caused by accidental contact with the board, the platform, or the bottom of the pool. In competitive diving, most such injuries occur when the diver is attempting an inward or backward dive, such as the ones Louganis and Chalibashvili were attempting, and does not get out far enough from the board or platform. Other injuries, such as neck strain, sprains in the wrists or hands, or even a dislocated shoulder, can occur from hitting the surface of the water improperly.

Hitting the diving board or platform is also the most common cause of diving injuries among amateur and recreational swimmers, especially among children, teens, and young adults. A 2008 research study conducted by the Center for Injury Research and Policy (CIRP) of the Research Institute at Nationwide Children's Hospital in Columbus, Ohio, found that injuries were most common among children ages ten to fourteen. Gary Smith, a physician at Nationwide Children's Hospital says, "Every year in this country, approximately 6,500 children are treated in emergency departments for diving related injury."[18] Cuts and bruises are the most common injuries, with the head, face, and neck the most commonly injured area. The study also shows that boys are taken to the hospital with diving injuries twice as much as girls and that injuries are most common during backwards dives or dives that include flips or handstands.

The most serious diving injuries occur when a person dives head first into water that is too shallow. Sudden, hard contact with the bottom of a swimming pool or the bottom of a shallow lake or river can result in a severe head injury or a fractured neck. Like drowning, head and neck injuries from diving are much more common in boys and young men, usually because of careless or reckless behavior or diving while impaired by alcohol or drugs.

A blow to the head can cause a skull fracture or bleeding into the brain, which may not be discovered until the person develops symptoms. Symptoms of a head injury, or concussion, may include nausea with vomiting, slurred speech, clumsiness, or decreased consciousness. Severe head injuries with damage to the brain or bleeding into the brain can cause coma or death.

If the impact causes the head to be forced downward toward the shoulders, or bent or twisted in an unnatural direction, the delicate spinal cord in the cervical spine can be damaged. A spinal cord injury may be complete or incomplete. In a complete spinal cord injury, messages from the brain cannot be sent to the body below the level of the injury. A spinal cord damaged this badly cannot be repaired, and permanent paralysis from the point of the injury down is the result. This is called quadriplegia. The person with quadriplegia may be unable to breathe on his or her own, may not be able to control bowel or bladder function, and will not be able to feel or move anything below the point of the injury. If the spinal cord injury is incomplete, the injured person may still have some function in one or more parts of the body below the injury or may have more function on one side of the body than the other.

Lara McKenzie, coauthor of the Nationwide Children's Hospital study, stresses that "there is a need for increased prevention efforts to lower the risks of diving-related injuries among children and adolescents. The recent growth of the sport of diving, coupled with the increasing complexity and difficulty of dives, has resulted in a greater potential for both competitive and recreational diving-related injuries."[19]

CHAPTER 4

The Physics of Swimming

S wimming is the only sport in which the athlete moves through something other than air. The swimmer must also keep him- or herself off the ground for the duration of his or her event. Moving quickly through water and staying afloat involve some rather complex principles of science, in particular, the science of physics. Physics studies the relationships in nature between matter, energy, time, motion, and forces such as gravity and buoyancy. All these factors are involved in the physics of swimming.

Isaac Newton and Swimming

Seventeenth-century-physicist Sir Isaac Newton made many observations about physical forces at work in nature and developed ideas about how they work together and relate to each other. Newton is probably most famous for his ideas about gravity, which, according to legend, he "discovered" after being hit on the head by an apple falling from a tree. Newton was also interested in how objects behave when they are in motion. He came up with three laws which are referred to today as Newton's Laws of Motion. All three of these laws, although four hundred years old, can be applied to swimming today.

Newton's first law of motion is the Law of Inertia. In physics, inertia is the tendency of an object to resist being moved or changed. Newton's first law has two parts, each of which pertains to one of two types of inertia. Static inertia means that an object at rest will stay at rest unless it is acted upon by an outside force. For example, if a swimmer floats in the water, his or her body will not move unless the swimmer kicks, takes an arm stroke, pushes off from the wall or bottom of the pool, or is moved along by movement of the water itself (outside forces). The second kind of inertia is dynamic inertia. This means that an object in motion will continue to move in a straight line unless acted upon by an outside force. Once a swimmer pushes off the side of the pool and begins to move forward, he or she will continue to move forward until the resistance of the water (the outside force) slows the swimmer down.

Newton's second law is the Law of Acceleration. This law states that the speed of a moving object depends on the mass of the object (how much matter is contained in the object) and on how much force is applied to the object to make it

Sir Isaac Newton's Laws of Motion come into play as swimmers push off from the side of the pool during a lap turn in a race.

move. This law can be expressed in a simple mathematical equation: Force equals Mass multiplied by Acceleration, or

$$F = M \times A$$

This equation means several things. It means that an object will move faster if more force is applied to it. For example, if two swimmers have equal mass, the one who pushes off the wall of the pool harder or has a stronger arm stroke (more force) will move faster (greater acceleration) than the swimmer who applies less force. The equation also means that if two objects of different masses are acted upon by the same amount of force, the one with less mass will move faster than the one with more mass. For swimmers, it means that a bigger swimmer (greater mass) needs to push off the wall harder (more force) in order to go as fast as a smaller swimmer.

The third law of motion is the Law of Action and Reaction, also called the Law of Force Pairs. It states that for every action, there is an equal and opposite reaction. It means that whenever a force is applied to an object in one direction, there is an equal amount of force applied in the opposite direction. There are many examples of this in nature. When a frog jumps off a lily pad, his legs push himself forward (the action) and the lily pad backward (the opposite reaction). The harder he pushes, the farther he goes forward and the farther the lily pad goes backward. When a swimmer takes an arm stroke, he or she pushes water backwards and down (action). This pushes the swimmer forward and up (opposite reaction). The more powerful the stroke, the farther the swimmer goes with each stroke. This is the swimmer's "distance per stroke," or DPS. Elite swimmers and their trainers who understand this law pay a lot of attention to measuring the swimmer's DPS.

The Force of Gravity

In addition to his three laws of motion, Newton also developed the Law of Gravity. He defined gravity as a downward force that exerts a pull on all objects. Gravity can be seen at work every day. It is what causes a stone to fall to the ground when dropped, and it is what keeps people and objects from floating off into space. Gravity keeps the moon in its orbit around Earth and Earth in its orbit around the sun, and it is what causes objects (such as swimmers) to sink into the water.

The force of gravity is greater on objects that have greater mass. Mass is related to weight, but mass and weight are not the same thing. Mass is a measure of how much matter an object contains. Weight is a measure of how much gravity is exerted on an object. A bowling ball has the same amount of mass on the moon as it does on Earth, but because the moon has less mass than Earth, it has less of a gravitational pull, so the ball weighs less on the moon. Mass also has little to do with size. A feather pillow is larger than a brick, but the brick has more mass. Gravity pulls harder on it, so it weighs more than the pillow.

The force of gravity is lessened when objects are far apart. An astronaut in space has the same amount of mass that he does on Earth, but because he is so far away, he is not subject to Earth's gravitational pull, and he becomes weightless. If he lands on the moon, he becomes subject to the moon's gravitational pull, but just like the bowling ball, he weighs less on the moon than he does on Earth because the gravitational pull of the moon is less.

Archimedes' Principle and Buoyancy

Another physical concept called buoyancy is involved when objects are contained in fluid (a liquid or a gas). It explains why a small pebble sinks in water, while a battleship, which is considerably heavier, does not. Buoyancy is what helps battleships, as well as swimmers, overcome gravity and stay afloat.

The concept of buoyancy was first described by Archimedes (about 287 B.C–212 B.C), a Greek mathematician, astronomer, and philosopher. In the third century B.C., King Hiero of Syracuse (on the Mediterranean island of Sicily) became suspicious that the goldsmith who had made his crown had made it, not from the pure gold he had been given from the treasury, but from a cheaper blend of gold and silver, and that he had kept the leftover gold for himself. At that time, however, there was no way to determine exactly how much of the crown was gold and how much, if any, was silver.

The king gave the problem to Archimedes. Archimedes already knew that silver had less mass than gold and that it would take more silver than gold to weigh a given amount. He knew that a crown that contained silver would have to be somewhat larger than a solid gold crown in order for it to weigh as much as the gold that the goldsmith had been given. Before Archimedes could determine how much of the crown was gold and how much was silver, he would need to determine the volume of the crown—the total amount of metal the crown contained. But there was no way to determine the volume of the crown without melting it down and shaping it into a basic shape, like a sphere or a cube, for which volume formulas already existed, and Archimedes knew that the king would not be happy with that.

One day, while Archimedes was sitting in a bath, he observed how the level of the water rose when he got in and lowered when he got out. He understood that his body mass was displacing, or moving, a volume of water equal to the volume of his body. He realized then that the volume of any object, including a crown, could be measured by measuring the amount of water displaced by the object. Using the volume and the weight of the crown, Archimedes could prove that the crown had less mass than an equal volume of pure gold. He demonstrated this by hanging the crown and an equal volume of pure gold from a scale and lowering them into water. In the water, the gold sank lower than the crown, proving that the crown had less mass than the pure gold and, therefore, was made at least partially from another substance, presumably silver.

Archimedes used this new knowledge to formulate what has become known as Archimedes' Principle, which states that a fluid, such as water, exerts an upward force on an object that helps to counteract the force of gravity. This force is called buoyancy. The amount of buoyancy exerted on an object is equal to the weight of the amount of water displaced by the object. If an object weighs more than the amount of water it displaces, it is called negatively buoyant, and it will sink. If it weighs less than the displaced water, it is positively buoyant, and it will float. If it weighs the same as the displaced water, it is called neutrally buoyant, and the object will neither sink nor float, but will remain suspended in the water. Also, an object such as a cork, which contains air, is less dense and will float,

BUOYANT FORCE

According to Archimedes' Principle, the buoyant force exerted on an object is equal to the weight of the water that it displaces. If the weight of the displaced water is greater than that of the object, and the object has less density than the surrounding water, the object will float because the buoyant force on the object will be greater than the force of gravity.

Little girl weighs 50 lbs.

She floats because the **buoyant force** is greater than her body weight and her body is less dense than the surrounding water.

55 lbs.

| Weight of displaced water | = | buoyant force |

because air is so light in weight, but an airless and denser rock of the same size will sink. This is why a battleship can float when a pebble does not. A battleship, which is made largely of air-filled rooms, displaces a volume of water that weighs more than the ship itself, so it floats. The pebble, on the other hand, displaces a very small amount of water that weighs less than the pebble, so the pebble sinks. (If the ship were to get a hole in its hull under the water level, the air in the ship would be replaced by heavier water, and the ship would eventually sink.)

The buoyancy exerted on a swimmer's body varies from swimmer to swimmer. Human bodies vary in mass depending on their composition. Bone and muscle have more mass than fat. Women tend to be more buoyant than men, because their bones tend to be smaller and because their bodies have a higher proportion of fat than a man's. Children tend to be more buoyant than adults for the same reasons. Buoyancy is also increased when a deep breath is taken and the lungs are filled with air because air decreases the total density of the body and helps it float.

Buoyancy and Salt Water

Buoyancy is the upward force exerted by a fluid on an object in the fluid. If the weight of the fluid displaced by the object weighs more than the object, the object will float. The denser the fluid, the more it weighs, and the more likely an object is to float in it.

If a cube weighing 63 pounds (29kg) and measuring 1 foot (30cm) on each side (a cubic foot) is put into fresh water, it displaces 1 cubic foot of water, which weighs only 62.4 pounds (28.3kg). Since the cube weighs more than the water it displaces, the cube will sink. Because of the salt and other minerals which are dissolved in ocean water, however, a cubic foot of ocean water weighs 64 pounds (29kg). Therefore, the 63-pound (28.6kg) cube will float in ocean water. The more salt and minerals that are dissolved in water, the more buoyant an object will be. It is easier for a swimmer to stay afloat in ocean water than in fresh water because of its greater buoyancy.

Resistance and Drag

Like gravity, resistance, or drag, is a physical force that a swimmer must overcome in order to move efficiently through the water. Because water is a liquid, its molecules are packed much closer together than air molecules, so water is much denser than air. A person moving through water is slower than a person moving through air, because the water exerts resistance against a person's body and against his or her efforts to move through it.

There are four types of resistance acting upon a swimmer: frontal resistance, form drag, skin friction, and eddy resistance. Frontal resistance is resistance that is exerted on the swimmer by the water in front of his or her body. The more of the body's surface area that is in contact with the water, the more frontal resistance there is. Swimmers try to overcome frontal resistance by adopting a posture in the water that keeps as much of their body above the surface of the water as possible. Raising the head up during breathing tends to cause the lower body to sink slightly in the water, which exposes more body surface to the water, so swimmers try to keep their head as close as possible to the surface when they turn it to take a breath. Rolling the body slightly from side to side as the swimmer uses arm strokes also helps raise the body and keep it higher in the water, which helps reduce frontal resistance.

Closely related to frontal resistance is form drag. Form drag refers to the shape, or form, of the object that is moving through the water. An object with a more irregular shape meets more frontal resistance in the water than a more streamlined object. This is one reason why fish, sharks, and dolphins are much faster swimmers than animals such as dogs or elephants. Their bodies are narrow, smooth, and streamlined, so they can move in the water with much less resistance. When a swimmer dives into the water from the starting block, he or she extends the arms forward with the hands together, keeps the head down, and keeps the feet together with toes pointed.

A competitive swimmer wears a specially-designed swimsuit with a surface that reduces friction in the water, thus improving speed.

This reduces form drag and allows the swimmer to enter the water with much less resistance.

The third kind of resistance, skin friction, is resistance caused by water flowing over the surface of the swimmer's body. Whenever two surfaces, such as water and the swimmer's skin, move against each other, friction is created. Friction tends to slow objects down as they move. The rougher or more irregular the surfaces are, the more friction is created. For example, a

Lift vs Drag

While it is commonly accepted among swimming scientists that both lift and drag forces contribute to the overall force of the swimming stroke, there is still considerable debate among swimming experts about which force contributes more to swimming success. With the 1968 publication of swimming scientist and coach James Counsilman's work, *The Science of Swimming,* lift became the most widely accepted source of propulsive force in swimming, rather than drag, and coaches taught their swimmers to use the sculling action of the hand. Throughout the 1980s and 1990s, many studies were conducted to determine which force actually contributes most.

Those who support drag as the more important force point out that the forearm, with its mostly round shape and unchanging angle of movement through the water, generates almost exclusively drag force. Others point out that the shape of the arm stroke is actually less curved than earlier thought and that it is mainly a result of the body rolling from side to side during the swim, rather than due to a deliberate action by the swimmer. Proponents of lift forces feel that the forearm contribution to force is not important compared to the hand because the hand moves at a much higher speed than the forearm. Other studies have concluded that the relative contribution of each force changes throughout the stroke and that it depends on the angle of the hand relative to the direction of the water.

Scientists have studied the arm and hand position of a swimmer's stroke to determine whether lift or drag is the dominant propulsive force.

baseball rolls slower on grass than it does on dirt because the grass is rougher and puts more friction on the ball. Swimmers use various methods to reduce skin friction. They may shave the hair off of any part of the skin that comes in contact with water (even the eyebrows) to make the skin surface smoother. Open-water swimmers may cover the skin with lotion or a lubricant, such as petroleum jelly.

Today's high-tech racing suits are designed to reduce friction by mimicking the structure of sharkskin. They have tiny V-shaped ridges along them designed to help direct water backward along the swimmer's body. They also compress the muscles and limit muscle movement, or "wobble," that is not directly required for propulsion. The suits are just one way in which technology has influenced competitive swimming. "World swimming has moved on," says Michael Scott, the national performance director for British Swimming, the national governing body for swimming in Great Britain. "The world has become more competitive. It's a combination of a variety of factors and technology is playing a part in that."[20]

The fourth type of resistance is called eddy resistance, or wave resistance. This type of resistance is caused by the turbulence created as the swimmer uses arm strokes and leg kicks. Turbulent water moving against a swimmer exerts more resistance on the swimmer. Poor stroke technique tends to create more eddy resistance. It is also caused by turbulence created by other swimmers in the pool. The ropes between racing lanes help to minimize the effect of waves on nearby swimmers by breaking up the waves. Wave resistance created by natural waves, water currents, and weather conditions is a particularly important factor for open-water swimmers, especially those swimming in the ocean.

Passive and Active Drag

The types of drag felt by a swimmer as he or she moves through the water are referred to as passive drag. They are passive because the swimmer does not exert the resistance

on the water; the water exerts the resistance on the swimmer. Another kind of drag is called active drag. Active drag is drag that the swimmer exerts on the water each time he or she takes a stroke. This type of drag is an example of Newton's Third Law of Motion and, unlike passive drag, actually acts to the swimmer's advantage. As a swimmer takes a stroke, he or she pushes backward against the resistance of the water. This movement propels the swimmer forward. The more powerful the stroke, the greater the active drag on the water, and the more efficiently the swimmer moves forward.

Until the 1970s, swimmers were taught to reach into the water with the palm facing straight down and to pull the water straight back, that is, to use active drag forces. In the late 1960s, pioneering swimming scientist and Indiana University swimming coach James "Doc" Counsilman, found that the most successful swimmers were those who used a

Sculling, a figure-eight type movement with the hands, is used by synchronized swimmers to hold their bodies in position in the water.

STARTING BLOCK

23

The number of swimming records broken at the 2008 Olympics by swimmers wearing the Speedo LZR Racer swimsuit.

"sculling" movement with the hands. Sculling is a back-and-forth, figure-eight type movement of the arms and hands that creates increased propulsive (or forward moving) forces as the hand pushes against the water. When a person treads water, the body is aligned vertically in the water. The swimmer uses arms and hands in a sculling fashion to move water downward, which helps keep the body upward and helps keep the head above the water. A swimmer, whose body is aligned horizontally in the water, also uses a sculling motion during each stroke to move forward more efficiently than with a straight backward movement. Sculling is a particularly important skill in synchronized swimming, because it helps the athlete control body position in the water, especially when the head is down.

One reason for the advantage of a sculling motion is that when the hand takes a curved path through the water, rather than a straight path, more water is "caught" and pushed backward, thereby propelling the swimmer forward with more force. Another reason that sculling improves a swimmer's performance has to do with another physical property—lift.

The Bernoulli Principle and Lift Forces

Daniel Bernoulli (1700–1782) was a Dutch mathematician who is known for applying mathematics to the study of fluid mechanics. In 1738, he published his book *Hydrodynamica*, in which he describes what has become known as Bernoulli's Principle. Simply expressed, Bernoulli's Principle states that as the speed of a fluid stream increases, the pressure in the stream decreases. The most common example of this is seen in the wing of an airplane. The top surface of the wing is curved, and the bottom is flat. Also, the front, or leading, edge of the wing is thicker than the back, or trailing, edge. This kind of shape is called a foil. In order to cover the longer distance over the top of the wing, air (which in science is considered to be "fluid" and

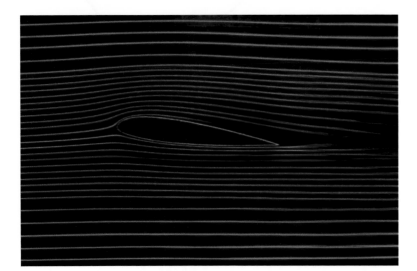

Bernoulli's principle is illustrated by the change in shape of fluid lines as they travel over and under a wing-shaped foil. Swimmers apply this principle to determine optimal hand position during a stroke.

behave in the same ways as a liquid, like water) must move faster across the top than it does along the flat bottom of the wing. As the air moves faster over the top of the wing, the pressure it exerts on the wing is less than the pressure exerted by the air under the wing. With less pressure over the wing than under it, the wing is lifted upward.

The same principle can be applied to a swimmer's hand as it makes a sculling movement through the water. The top surface of the hand is more curved than the bottom surface. In addition, the thumb side of a hand is thicker than the little finger side of the hand. The hand, therefore, has a foil-like shape and moves through water like an airplane wing moves through air.

In a straight-back kind of stroke, the hand enters the water flat and pulls the water straight backward, using only active drag forces. In a sculling movement, however, the hand enters the water with the thumb side angled slightly downward. This kind of hand position uses the foil shape of the hand to produce a Bernoulli-like effect to generate the same kind of lift forces on the swimmer that are created on an airplane. This combination of lift forces with drag forces increases the total force produced by the hand, which increases the speed of the water being pushed backward and helps to propel the swimmer forward with more speed, an example of Newton's Second Law of Motion.

CHAPTER 5

The Psychology of Swimming

S wimming is unique among sports because everyone from infants to the elderly can enjoy the benefits of swimming. People, unlike most other mammals, however, do not have the instinctive ability to swim; they must be taught. Learning to swim involves more than just mastering basic skills, such as arm strokes and leg kicks. People also have to learn to adapt to the buoyancy of water—the sensation of being off the ground. The water environment, since it is not a natural environment for people, carries with it certain dangers, and people must learn to overcome a natural anxiety about being in and under the water.

At the competitive level, swimmers must learn to deal with the stress of competition and the pressure to win. They have to cope with emotions involved with losing or with getting injured, such as anger and frustration. Competitive swimmers must also learn to cope with the pressures of maintaining their success and with media attention. How a swimmer trains the mind is as important as how he or she trains the body.

Learning to Swim

According to the Centers for Disease Control and Prevention (CDC) in Atlanta, Georgia, and the American Academy of Pediatrics (AAP), drowning is the second-leading cause

Children make their way across the pool with the help of kickboards during a swimming lesson. Learning to swim can improve a child's cognitive, motor, and social skills.

of death in children between the ages of one and nineteen. Despite this statistic, in 2004, the AAP issued the opinion that children under the age of four should not be taught how to swim. The AAP reasoned that children under age four do not retain skills they have learned and parents may believe that their children can swim when they actually cannot and may not supervise them as closely as they should.

Groups of water safety professionals, such as the United States Swim School Association (USSSA) and the Swim for

Life Foundation, disagreed with the AAP. They cited research that showed that swimming and water safety classes for children in that age group may decrease drowning. In 2010 the AAP revised its recommendations to include swimming lessons for healthy young children over age one.

Learning to swim at a young age has developmental benefits in addition to improving safety around the water. As children are exposed to new experiences, the experiences and the information learned from them are recorded and stored in the brain. The brain of a young child adapts very quickly to new information and can use it later in other situations in which the learned information might be useful. Participation in organized learning activities that include movement, such as swimming lessons, improves a child's ability to focus on tasks and enhances his or her overall ability to learn. It also improves a child's self-esteem and confidence in his or her own abilities.

A young child who learns to adapt his or her body to the movement and buoyancy of water learns motor skills, such as coordination and spatial awareness (understanding where the body and its parts are in relation to each other and the space around it), which the child can use later in other situations, such as other sports. Children over the age of five who have not already learned these adaptations at a younger age may have more trouble developing the physical skills needed to swim well and be safe in the water. They may also struggle with the sensation of lower gravity in the water and may develop a fear of the water that must be overcome before they can learn to swim. Fear of water is a psychological condition known as aquaphobia.

Aquaphobia

When Ted Sherman was six years old, he had a frightening experience that stayed with him the rest of his life. He recalls,

> I had waded in the ocean several times, but I had never been in a swimming pool before. As we marched in line

along the poolside, another kid pushed me in. I was so frightened, I just flailed my arms as I sank under several times. While the other kids laughed, an instructor jumped in and hauled me out. I couldn't have been in the water alone more than thirty seconds, but I was sure I was drowning. What also made the other kids laugh was that the water was in the shallow end of the pool, and all I had to do was stand up, and my head would have been out of the water. My panic was real, and if the instructor had not saved me, I could actually have drowned in less than three feet of water.[21]

Ted eventually learned to swim and overcame his fear of the water. He was a champion swimmer in high school and taught water safety in the navy during World War II.

Many people who cannot swim (and even some who can) have a fear of the water, or aquaphobia, from the Latin word *aqua* (water) and the Greek word *phobos* (fear). Aquaphobia may be mild, with the main symptom being a lack of confidence in the water, or it may be so severe as to interfere with daily life. A person with severe aquaphobia may not be able to take baths, wade in shallow water, or even tolerate being splashed with water or being in the rain. The fear of water is often uncontrollable and persists even though the person consciously realizes that the water itself poses no real threat.

Aquaphobia can be caused in several ways. The person may have had an unpleasant or frightening experience in the water, like Ted Sherman. A person may develop a fear of water after witnessing someone else drown or almost drown, or from watching a frightening movie involving water, such as *Jaws* or *Titanic*. They may learn to fear the water from a parent who

Sport Psychology

Sport psychology is the study of how participation in sports and exercise affects the mental and emotional health of people and how mental and emotional factors affect the competitive athlete's performance. It involves teaching psychological skills, such as emotional control, self-talk, visualization, confidence, goal setting, and relaxation, to improve an athlete's performance.

Sport psychologists are psychologists who specialize in athletes. One of the first sport psychologists was Norman Triplett (1861–1931), who found through his research that cyclists do better when they ride in pairs or groups rather than alone. In the 1920s psychologists in Germany and the United States established sport psychology laboratories and began to teach sport psychology. In the 1970s, sport psychology became a common component of sports training at colleges and universities. Today, sport psychologists may work directly with athletes, teaching mental training techniques. They may work in an office helping athletes to overcome psychological stumbling blocks, such as depression, loss of confidence, substance abuse, or eating disorders. They may also work in an academic setting, such as a university, in which the focus is on research and teaching new sport psychologists.

is also afraid of it. A person with aquaphobia may go to great lengths to avoid being near water. When near water, the person may develop symptoms similar to a panic attack, such as fast heartbeat, difficulty breathing, uncontrollable shaking, or abdominal pain.

Aquaphobia can be overcome, and there are several ways to treat it. Working with an experienced and patient swimming instructor or lifeguard can help the person with aquaphobia learn to be more relaxed and less fearful around water. Taking "baby steps" and gradually increasing contact with water helps build confidence. Relaxation techniques, such as deep breathing, can decrease anxious feelings. Psychologists can also help people overcome their fear of the water by using cognitive behavioral therapy, a technique that helps people learn new ways to cope with the fear and to replace negative thoughts about water with more positive ones. Especially severe cases may require medication.

STARTING BLOCK
Water phobias
Aquaphobia is a fear of water. Cymphobia is a fear of waves. Ablutophobia is a fear of bathing.

Psychology and Competitive Swimming

Baseball legend Yogi Berra is credited with saying, "Ninety percent of [baseball] is half mental." While the quote sounds humorous, he is right that what goes on in the mind of an athlete (the "inside game") is just as important, if not more important, than what goes on in the body (the "outside game"). The inside game has to do with the athletes' mental approach to their performance. It has to do with their beliefs about their abilities; their confidence in themselves and their team; and their ability to concentrate, focus, and deal with pressure and failure. "The mind body connection is a very powerful one," says sport psychologist Karlene Sugarman. "For everything you think in your mind, your body has a reaction, regardless of whether it is real or imagined. ... With this premise, it becomes unmistakable how necessary it is to train both the mind and the body for peak performance."[22]

Swimmers and their coaches spend a great deal of time training the body and practicing physical skills that will give

A coach monitors a swimmer's technique during practice. In addition to the development of physical skills, swimmers must also prepare mentally in order to handle the demands of training and competition.

them the slightest edge over their opponents. Although they may be aware of how important mental training is, often not enough attention is paid to that aspect of training. As Sugarman says, "most athletes fatigue mentally before they fatigue physically, due to the fact that their mind is not in as good of shape as their bodies."[23]

Sport psychologist Aimee Kimball stresses how important it is for the swimmer to know what kind of mental state, or mindset, he or she functions best in and then take steps to achieve that mental state. "Every individual has a unique mental state under which he or she performs best," she says. "There is not one right way to think. The key is to know what you are thinking and how you are feeling when you perform your best."[24] She suggests that athletes develop a routine to follow before each performance to help recreate that mindset and that they choose a "trigger" word that is meaningful to them that will remind them to think that way. Getting into the best mindset helps athletes feel confident and focused and helps them control nervousness and anxiety before a competition.

Competition Anxiety

Anxiety is a natural response to a stressful situation or event that may be perceived as a threat. It is part of the basic "fight or flight" response to danger or potential harm, instinctive in most animals as well as people. Anxiety causes the heart rate to increase, the breathing to quicken, the muscles to tense, and the pupils of the eye to open wider. All these responses prepare the animal or person to either fight the threat or flee from it.

Athletic competition can be seen as a threat, but not so much as a physical danger as a psychological one. The potential for failure is a threat to anyone's ego and self-esteem. If an athlete believes that the demands of the competition are greater than his or her ability, anxiety is the result. At the highest levels of swimming competition, such as the Olympics, the pressure to succeed is enormous. The stakes are high, and there is very little room for error. Competitions are won and lost in thousandths of a second, and the outcome of an event is uncertain. The athlete must often perform in front of hundreds or thousands of spectators, and the audience could be in the millions if the event is broadcast on television. High-level competition can be physically demanding and exhausting. All these things can cause anxiety, especially for swimmers, who compete mostly in events in which the attention is on individual athletes rather than on an entire team.

Anxiety by itself is not necessarily a harmful thing. It creates a heightened sense of awareness of one's surroundings. It leads an athlete to be more alert and more focused. It can be a

STAYING ORIENTED

The brain uses three mechanisms to help orient the body within its surrounding environment: the sense of touch through the nervous system (spinal cord, nerves), visual cues received through the eyes, and a sense of balance arising from the force of gravity on fluid structures in the inner ear. Swimmers can sometimes become disoriented and experience severe dizziness, known as vertigo, as a result of physical sensory overload, visual impairment, or pressure changes in the inner ear.

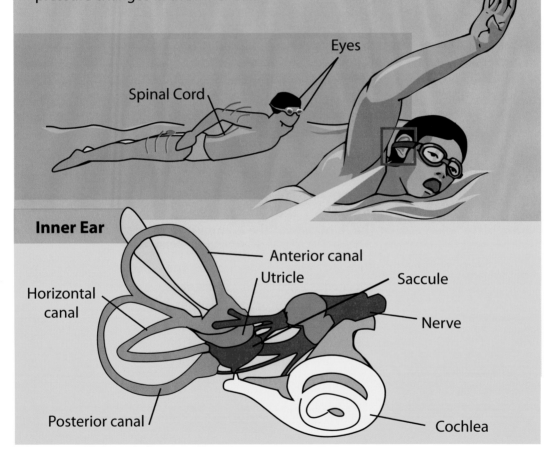

Eyes

Spinal Cord

Inner Ear

Anterior canal

Utricle

Saccule

Horizontal canal

Nerve

Posterior canal

Cochlea

very motivating and energizing feeling. It is only when anxiety becomes uncontrolled and overwhelms the athlete that it can be harmful. Some athletes get so anxious right before competing that they actually become ill. Competition anxiety

Measuring Competition Anxiety

It is well-known that anxiety plays a significant role in an athlete's ability to perform well. Sport psychologists have attempted to find a way to reliably measure athletes' tendency to feel anxiety and their individual response to it. In 1990 three sport psychologists developed a fifteen-item questionnaire called the Sport Competition Anxiety Test (SCAT) that was specifically designed for athletes and focused on two types of anxiety. Cognitive anxiety is what an athlete thinks and believes about competition and how he or she responds to it mentally. It includes such things as indecision, negative self-talk, poor concentration, and irritability. Somatic anxiety is how the athlete's body reacts physically to stress and includes symptoms such as a pounding heart, sweating, nausea, and pacing. The 2003 Competitive State Anxiety Inventory, or CSAI-2R, is another questionnaire used for measuring competitive anxiety in athletes. It includes seventeen statements that also measures cognitive and somatic anxiety but adds a measurement of self-confidence, or how sure the athlete feels about his or her own abilities. Today, the CSAI-2R is the most commonly used tool for assessing an athlete's competition anxiety and his or her responses to it.

can cause an athlete to "freeze" just when he or she needs to perform. It can cause the athlete to make mistakes that he or she would normally never make. All these things interfere with a swimmer's ability to achieve peak performance.

Be "In the Zone"

The goal of any athlete, including swimmers, is to achieve peak performance. When athletes perform at their peak, they feel that they can do nothing wrong and that everything is going their way. Everything they do just seems to happen with very little effort and with no interference from distracting thoughts or feelings. When athletes perform at their peak, they are said to be "in the zone."

Swimmer Misty Hyman, an Olympic gold medalist, describes what being "in the zone" was like for her just before her 200-meter butterfly event in the 2000 Olympics:

Everything went so smoothly. I don't remember the events of the finals exactly. I know that I was definitely

Gold medalist Misty Hyman competes in the 2000 Summer Olympic Games. She credits her mental focus as a key component of her competitive success.

in the moment, and I wasn't thinking too much. I was doing what I needed to do. ... I remember being able to feel every cell in my body and be completely present. Things felt like they were in slow motion. I dove in the water and it just clicked. I felt more power than ever before.[25]

Relaxation Techniques

The swimmer who is feeling "in the zone" is relaxed. Energy level is high, and the swimmer feels excited and a little nervous but not overly anxious, jittery, or physically ill. The swimmer who is "in the zone" is in control of anxiety, alert, and focused. Many swimmers take time before an event to perform relaxation techniques. Meditation, imagery, self-talk, music, and hypnosis are all methods that can be used to achieve relaxation and control anxiety.

Meditation is a holistic technique, meaning it has benefits for the mind, the body and the spirit of the person. It was developed by Tibetan monks over two thousand years ago. Meditation involves training the mind to focus one's attention on a particular desired internal state of mind, eliminating all external distractions and gaining control over one's own thoughts and attitudes. Done regularly, meditation helps the person achieve a state of relaxation and calmness. It is best done in a quiet, dimly lit location with no distractions or interruptions. Meditation is helpful for many athletes, because it helps them release stress; think positively instead of negatively; become calm, relaxed, and more focused; and achieve their ideal mindset for performance.

Imagery

Imagery, or visualization, is a very powerful technique for an athlete to use before competition. The mind cannot make the distinction between something that is actually happening and something that a person is imagining and visualizing in their head. This is why a person might awaken from a nightmare gasping for breath and sweating with the heart

A swimmer takes a moment before a race to focus his thoughts and visualize his performance. Such techniques help an athlete mentally prepare for competition.

racing. The mind believes the dream to be real. Imagery is a conscious way of creating an image of a desired event in the mind, such as winning a race. It is a way to achieve in the mind what the swimmer wants his or her body to do during the event. It is almost like creating a custom-made dream and then recreating that dream in real life.

Several senses can be included in imagery. While picturing the event in the mind, the athlete imagines what he or she is hearing, feeling, smelling, and even tasting. Imagery, like dreams, can either be internal, in which the athlete is the one actually performing, or external, in which the athlete imagines watching a video of himself or herself performing. Imagery requires regular practice in order to get good at it, but it can be very valuable for building confidence and controlling anxiety.

Self-Talk

Self-talk, also called internal monologue, is just what it sounds like—talking with oneself, either out loud or in the head—to build a mindset of confidence. It focuses on using positive words to boost self-esteem and to help athletes believe that they can do what they set out to do. Hyman used this technique before her butterfly event. "When standing on the blocks," she says, "I just said to myself, 'Ok, I'm going to do a 200 butterfly, and I've done a million 200 butterflies in my life. I have been training for this and I know exactly what I need to do.'"[26] Having this dialogue with herself helped Hyman stay positive and focused on her goal.

Self-talk can be used during practice sessions, to keep motivated and to focus on improving stroke technique, or it can be used to boost confidence before a performance, overcome fatigue during a performance, or review ways to improve in future performances. It can also be used to help shut out distractions, such as other swimmers, spectators, minor aches and pains, or other concerns not related to swimming.

Music and Motivation

Throughout history music has been an extremely powerful way to inspire and motivate people. It is used in religious rituals, political campaigns, concerts, sporting events,

movies, television programs and commercials, and in many other areas of life to invoke certain feelings and emotions in the listener. Many athletes use music to help motivate and relax themselves before an event and to unwind after an event. Swimmer Brendan Dedekind describes how music helps him: "When I am not excited for the race that is about to take place," he says, "listening to music alters my state of consciousness to be more 'excited' and hence helps me to perform at a higher level. It can also do the opposite, if the moment seems too big and I seem too nervous, listening to music can relax me and help me not to get too tense before a swim."[27] Music can bring back feelings the swimmer had during a previous good performance, improve sleep the night before a meet, or help shut out distractions.

Hypnosis

Hypnosis is a process in which the subconscious mind is accessed in a way that allows a person to shut out all distracting stimuli and focus on a particular goal or topic. It is not the same as the "hypnosis" that is portrayed in movies or on the stage, in which a hypnotist puts a person "to sleep" and makes him do things he would not otherwise do. A person under true hypnosis is not asleep at all and cannot be made to do anything he or she does not want to do. The person is actually wide-awake, but completely focused on only one thing to the exclusion of everything else. Hypnosis is somewhat similar to daydreaming, in which a person is so attentive to one thing that everything else is phased out of consciousness, but hypnosis goes deeper so that actual behavioral changes can be made. Scientists do not fully understand how hypnosis works, but its effects can be seen in those who have used it to quit smoking, lose weight, or achieve a desired goal.

Under hypnosis, a person is very relaxed and very suggestible, which means the mind is very receptive to ideas and suggestions. For athletes, hypnosis can help improve performance, because it can help the athlete control pain; improve self-confidence; focus entirely on goals; and eliminate anxiety, fear, and negative thoughts and emotions.

As in most sports, especially at the elite, competitive level, psychology has a major impact on the way an athlete performs. A positive mindset, including focus, determination, self-confidence, and a positive attitude, can make the difference between a champion and a runner-up. Athletes have a wide variety of psychological tools at their disposal to help them get in the zone and produce peak performance.

NOTES

Chapter 1: A Sport for the Ages

1. Herodotus. "The History of Herodotus." Translated by George Rawlinson. The Internet Classics Archive. http://classics.mit.edu/Herodotus/history.8.viii.html.
2. Egyptian State Information Service. "Ancient Egyptian Sport." Egyptian State Information Service. http://www.sis.gov.eg/En/Story.aspx?sid=1694.
3. Quoted in Mary Donahue. "History of Swimming Section." DeAnza College. http://faculty.deanza.edu/donahuemary/Historyofswimmingsection.
4. Quoted in International Swimming Hall of Fame. "Swimming from the Beginning." *Washington Post*. http://www.washingtonpost.com/wp-srv/sports/olympics/longterm/swimming/swimhist.htm.
5. John F. Walker. "Open Water Tips." Hulaman.com, April 18, 1995. www.hulaman.com/triathlon/open_wtr.html.
6. Quoted in Donahue. "History of Swimming Section."
7. Quoted in Donahue. "History of Swimming Section."

Chapter 2: Training and Conditioning

8. Quoted in Dennis McCafferty. "Swim Like Michael Phelps." *USA Weekend*, July 23–25, 2010, p. 16.
9. Gabe Mirkin. "How Muscles Get Stronger." DrMirkin.com. http://www.drmirkin.com/fitness/2056.html.
10. Mirkin. "How Muscles Get Stronger."
11. Quoted in Mat Luebbers. "Swimmers Can Improve Their Swimming Performance by Training Respiratory Muscles." About.com. http://swimming.about.com/od/swimmingscience/a/breath_training.htm.
12. Quoted in McCafferty. "Swim Like Michael Phelps."
13. Quoted in Jeré Longman and Gina Kolata. "Swimming Records Fall, Is There Something in the Water?" *New York Times*, August 11, 2008. http://www.nytimes.com/2008/08/11/sports/11iht-olyrecords.4.15182104.html.

Chapter 3: Injuries and Hazards

14. Jessica Seaton. "Is Your Swimming Giving You a Pain in the Neck?"

Chiropractic in West Los Angeles. http://www.drjessicaseaton.com/ Chiropractic_in_West_Los_Angeles/ Neck_Pain.html.

15. Bianca Diaz. "Back Injuries and Swimming." About.com. http://swimming.about.com/od/ injuryandrecovery/a/swim_back_ pain_2.htm.

16. Diaz. "Back Injuries and Swimming."

17. Quoted in Gerry Brown. "Louganis's Headache." Infoplease.com. http://www.infoplease.com/spot/ summer-olympics-greg-louganis .html.

18. Quoted in Science Daily. "First National Study of Diving-Related Injuries." Science Daily, August 6, 2008. http://www.sciencedaily.com/ releases/2008/08/080804100152 .htm.

19. Quoted in Science Daily. "First National Study of Diving Related Injuries."

Chapter 4: The Physics of Swimming

20. Quoted in Craig Lord. "Technology Transforming Swimming at Olympics." *Sunday Times*, August 10, 2008. http://www.timesonline .co.uk/tol/sport/olympics/ article4494267.ece.

Chapter 5: The Psychology of Swimming

21. Quoted in Ted Sherman. "Why Children Should Learn How to Swim When They Are Young." Helium, July 20, 2008. http://www .helium.com/items/1120098 -swim-lessons-for-toddlers.

22. Karlene Sugarman. "Why Mental Training?" Sports Psychology with Karlene Sugarman, M.A., January 4, 2007. http://www.psychwww .com/sports/mt.htm.

23. Sugarman. "Why Mental Training?"

24. Quoted in USA Swimming. "B Is for Building Your Mindset." USA Swimming. http://www.usaswimming. org/ViewMiscArticle.aspx? TabId=1595&Alias=Rainbow&Lan g=en&mid=9332&ItemId=4459.

25. Quoted in JoAnn Dahlkoetter. "Olympian Interviews." Your Performing Edge. http://www.sports-psych.com/interviews.html.

26. Quoted in Dahlkoetter. "Olympian Interviews."

27. Brendan Dedekind. "Motivation and the Place for Music in Swimming." About.com. http://swimming .about.com/od/sportpsychology/ qt/Music_Swimming_Motivation .htm.

GLOSSARY

active drag: Resistance that the swimmer creates in the water with each arm stroke.

aerobic: Cell functions that occur with oxygen.

anaerobic: Cell functions that occur without oxygen.

aquaphobia: Fear of the water.

Bernoulli principle: The principle that states that faster moving air exerts less pressure on an object than slower moving air, creating lift.

buoyancy: The upward pressure that a fluid exerts on an object that is in the fluid.

conduction: The transfer of heat from one molecule to another through a liquid.

convection: An increase in heat loss from an object in liquid when water is quickly moving around the object.

eddy resistance: The resistance exerted on a swimmer by water turbulence or waves.

force-velocity relationship: The relationship between force, mass, and speed of a moving object.

form drag: Resistance exerted on an object in a fluid that is dependent on the shape of the object.

frontal resistance: Resistance exerted on a swimmer by the water in front of his or her body.

gravity: The force that causes one object to pull toward another, especially the pull of Earth on all the objects on Earth.

hypothermia: A potentially dangerous health condition in which the body's core temperature is abnormally low.

impingement: A painful condition in which soft tissues are trapped between bony structures in a joint.

inertia: The tendency for objects at rest to remain at rest, or for objects in motion to remain in motion.

inflammation: Part of the body's immune response to illness or injury that causes swelling and pain.

instability: Looseness of the structures in a joint that allows the joint to move in abnormal ways.

lactate: A waste product of anaerobic metabolism that can cause fatigue and muscle weakness.

lactate threshold: During exercise, the point at which the waste product lactate builds up faster than the body's ability to eliminate it.

maximal oxygen uptake test (VO2): A test that measures the efficiency with which an athlete's body uses oxygen and eliminates metabolic waste products.

metabolic threshold: During exercise, the point at which the body begins to produce the waste product lactate.

metabolism: The chemical processes that occur within the body's cells in which fuel is used for cell function and growth.

passive drag: Resistance exerted against a swimmer by the water as he or she moves through it.

respiration: The act of breathing in and out. Also, the set of metabolic processes in which cells use oxygen and glucose to produce energy.

sculling: The curved, S-shaped movement of the hand as it enters the water and pulls backward during an arm stroke.

skin friction: The resistance exerted by objects as they move against each other.

volume: The amount of solid, liquid, or gas material that is contained in an object, or the amount of space taken up by an object.

FOR MORE INFORMATION

Books

Helene Boudreau. *Swimming Science.* New York: Crabtree, 2009. An introduction to the science involved in swimming.

Ian McLeod. *Swimming Anatomy.* Champagne, IL: Human Kinetics, 2009. An in-depth look at the muscles used in swimming and how to condition them for optimal performance.

Jason Page. *Swimming, Diving, and Other Water Sports.* New York: Crabtree, 2008. An overview of Olympic water sports.

David P. Torsiello. *Michael Phelps: Swimming for Olympic Gold.* Berkeley Heights, NJ: Enslow, 2009. A biography of American Olympic swimmer Michael Phelps.

Anne Wendorff. *Swimming.* Minneapolis, MN: Bellwether Media, 2010. A good introduction to the sport of swimming for younger readers.

Websites

Swimming World. (http://www .swimmingworldmagazine.com). A comprehensive source for news and information about swimming.

USA Swimming. (www.usaswimming .org). Provides information about training, conditioning, nutrition, and injury prevention for swimmers.

INDEX

A
Ablutophobia, 85
Acromioclavicular joint, 51
Acute injuries, 46–47
Aerobic endurance, 32, 34–37, *35*
Almásy, László, 13
Amateur Swimming Association of Great Britain, 16
American Red Cross water safety instructors, 82
Anabolic steroids, 36
Anaerobic metabolism, 37
Anaerobic training, 39
Anxiety, 87–89
Aquaphobia, 82–85, *83*
Archimedes, 69–70, *71, 72*
Ashmore, Linda, 21, 23
Australian crawl. *See* Front crawl

B
Babylonia, 14
Back injuries, 53–55, *54*
Backstroke, 12, 48
Base endurance training, 38
Bernoulli, Daniel, 78–79
Bernoulli Principle, 78–79, *79*
Body core temperature, 59
Body fat, percentage of, 32
Body orientation, *88*
Body roll, 10, 39–40
Boyton, Paul, 21
Breaststroke
    back pain, 53
    elements of, 12
    as first competitive stroke, 16–17
    knee injuries, 55, *56*
    in Middle Ages, 15
    neck pain and, 50
Breathing
    breaststroke, 12
    butterfly, *11*, 12
    front crawl, 10, 39–40
    muscles, *38*, 39, 40
    neck pain and, 49–50
    synchronized swimming, 25
    waste products removal, 35

Bridge diving, 24
Buoyancy, 70, *71,* 72
Butterfly, *11,* 12, 53

C
Cachexia, 44
Calcium, 45
Calories, 32, 42
Carbohydrates (carbs), 42–43
Cardiac muscle, 30
Cardiopulmonary resuscitation. *See* CPR
Catholic Church, opposition of, 14
Cavill, Richmond, 17
Cervical spine, 48, *49*
Chalibashvili, Sergei, 63
Children, teaching to swim, 81–82
Clavicle (collar bone), 51
Cold shock, 57
Cold water acclimatization, 57
Colymbetes (Wynman), 14–15
Competitions
    diving, 24
    history, 16–17
    mental preparation, 90–94, *91, 93*
    Ocean's Seven, 18
    for people with disabilities, 20, *21*
    psychology and, 84, 85–89
    synchronized swimming, 25–26
    water polo, 20
    See also Olympics (modern)
Competitive State Anxiety Inventory (CSAR-2R), 89
Conduction, losing heat through, 59, *60*
Convection, losing heat through, 59, *60*
Core muscles, strengthening, 30
CPR (cardio pulmonary resuscitation), 62
Critical Swim Speed test, 37
Cymphobia, 85

D
De arte natandi (Digby), 15
Dedekind, Brendan, *93,* 93–94
Dehydration, 44
Dickey, William, 17

PICTURE CREDITS

ABOUT THE AUTHOR

Lizabeth Hardman received her bachelor of science in nursing from the University of Florida in 1978 and her bachelor of science in secondary education from Southwest Missouri State University in 1991. She currently works full time as a surgical nurse.

Hardman has published both fiction and nonfiction for children and adults. *Swimming* is her ninth book for Lucent Books. She lives in Springfield, Missouri, with her two daughters, Rebecca and Wendy; two dogs; and three cats.